*Drama in a World of Science*

# Drama in a World of Science

## and three other lectures

by

GLYNNE WICKHAM

University of Toronto Press

TORONTO, 1962

.150746

Manufactured in Great Britain

For
H.D.F.K. and W.B.

# Contents

# Illustrations

*The illustrations are reproduced from photographs by Desmond Tripp (1 and 2) and by Roger Gilmour (3 and 4).*

# Preface

THE titles which appear as chapter headings in this book are those of four lectures. Each was given on a separate occasion and each in a different place; but all were prepared and delivered inside a year and deliberately related to one another in point of theme if not of circumstance.

The first, *Post-war Revolution in British Drama*, was prepared at the invitation of Professor Leighton Ballew, Head of the Department of Drama in the State University of Georgia. The second, *Poets and Playmakers*, was delivered at Cambridge in fulfilment of my obligation to the University as Judith E. Wilson Lecturer in Poetry and Drama. The third and fourth, *Drama in a World of Science* and *University Theatre*, were given respectively in Bristol and Nottingham. *University Theatre* was prepared at the invitation of Mr. John Holgate, President of the Society of Teachers of Speech and Drama, as an opening address for the society's Annual Conference. *Drama in a World of Science* was delivered as an inaugural address in my own University of Bristol. I have selected this lecture to serve as the collective title for the book, partly on that account and partly because its theme is the point of focus to which all the views expressed in the other lectures are related.

In the middle of the twentieth century the British theatre has arrived at a point of crisis where the gloomier prophets are predicting dissolution and death while the brighter optimists are proclaiming a refreshing renaissance and a future of remarkable vitality. As someone whose job confronts him daily with this crisis in two forms at once, practical and academic, I thought it worth while to examine its nature in some detail and record my findings in a manner which others could ponder and discuss in the light of their own experience and observation. That and that alone provides both the theme of these lectures and the relationship one to another.

We live in a world that is the product of scientific thinking and experiment. This is the world which our theatre must struggle to reflect and interpret if it is to be rated as possessing any cultural value worth preserving: yet it is a world which has itself lost faith in the cultural values inherited from the past. This is the crisis confronting the dramatist. The theatre's claim to serious attention rests in turn on its artists and their skill as mimetic interpreters. Yet the actor-manager system of recruiting and training gifted individuals has broken down and there is no agreement about an alternative training system. This is the crisis of the actor. Photography has placed the designer in a similar quandary, while films and television have elevated the director to a status among his collaborators of dubious application in theatrical art. And what of the audience? Rival attractions clamour for their attention, ranging from the most passive soporifics of television to the do-it-yourself activity of amateur dramatics. Has the public time to think or care what is happening to the professional theatre in their midst? It is here that the schools and universities ought to be supplying guidance; but it is questionable whether the guidance being actually offered amounts to more than blind men leading the blind.

These are some immediate causes of the crisis. If the prophets of doom are not to be proved right in the course of the latter half of this century, it is a matter of some urgency to take the measure of the crisis and act upon the knowledge gained: for unless we know where we are going and why, we shall lose our theatre as surely as the ancient Romans lost theirs—and for much the same reasons.

These lectures lay no claim to providing a systematic analysis of the crisis. They have served their purpose if they have directed attention to some aspects of it in which professionals, amateurs, and academics have mutual interests and which, if they choose to work together, they have it in their power to remedy.

GLYNNE WICKHAM

*Department of Drama, University of Bristol*

xii

# *Acknowledgements*

M Y thanks are due to Dr. C. A. Burch, F.R.S., and to Mr. George Brandt for their help in preparing these lectures for the printer.

The title and theme were suggested to me by the reading, some time ago, of the two Lewis Fry Memorial Lectures for 1928–9 delivered in the University of Bristol by Professor C. Lloyd Morgan, F.R.S., under the title *Science and Drama*. The six stanzas of verse quoted on pages 32–33 first came to my notice in the second of these lectures, and I have to thank Professor T. J. B. Spencer for identifying them as taken from Part II of Sir William Watson's 'England My Mother', printed in *Lachrymae Musarum* (1892), p. 64; also in *Selected Poems* (1903), p. 23.

The extract from Bertolt Brecht's *Gedichte aus dem Messing-kauf* printed on pages 55–56 is given here in the English translation by John Berger and Anna Bostock.

The extracts from Harold Pinter's *The Birthday Party* printed on pages 26–28 are reprinted from the edition of the play prepared by the Encore Publishing Company Ltd., 1959.

My thanks are also due to Professor Bruce Pattison for many helpful suggestions and comments.

# I

# The Post-War Revolution in British Drama*

BRITISH Theatre, with its knights and its dames so much in evidence on its playbills, may well strike nationals of other countries as still the most conservative and traditional in the world. Yet there is only one theatre building in regular use built earlier than 1800, and the very idea of a knighthood for an actor was itself a novelty when Henry Irving received his accolade from Queen Victoria less than seventy years ago.

A by-product of Victorian activity in theatre-building and of the 'respectability' which Irving's knighthood was interpreted as bestowing on the actor's profession—a very important by-product as subsequent events have shown—was the rapid development of dramatic activity in those perennial strongholds of conservatism, the universities of Oxford and Cambridge. It is important to remember this; for in our own time, when so many of the most widely publicized names in the commercial theatre are university graduates, it is easy to forget that the university dramatic activity of those early days was both amateur in origin and recognized as such. In Cambridge, at least, the name given to the dramatic society, The Amateur Dramatic Club, or A.D.C. as it is more usually called, took note of this fact. This by-product of the theatre's newly acquired respectability developed faster than

* A Lecture delivered in the State University of Georgia and in the University of California at Berkeley, 1960.

I

anyone could have imagined in the early years of this century. In the years immediately preceding the second world war the A.D.C. and the Marlowe Society at Cambridge and the O.U.D.S. and the E.T.C. at Oxford had come to be regarded by many as direct stepping-stones to a professional career for both actors and producers rather than as amateur groups addicted to this form of leisure recreation. In some respects therefore the post-war British theatre may reasonably be regarded as the strict sequel to the theatre of the immediate pre-war years: revolution is thus an inappropriate word to use in connection with it, or, if it is to be used, then it must be discussed in a pre-war rather than a post-war setting.

In other respects, however, this seeming continuity of development is more apparent in outward externals than in any inner reality. Admittedly we are still possessed of a theatre whose buildings are predominantly of Victorian and Edwardian design, a theatre populated with more knights and dames than ever before, a theatre dominated (at least in respect of the classical repertoire) by Oxford and Cambridge graduates who earned their first theatrical laurels on amateur, university stages. Yet something has happened since the war which has a flavour all its own and which is making everything in the theatre that has survived from pre-war days look vaguely old-fashioned: even the O.U.D.S. and the Marlowe have come to be labelled by students as 'square'. What has caused this change? Is it a change that can fairly be described as a revolution? True, there has been no 'forcible substitution by subjects of a new government or ruler for the old'—which is how the dictionary defines revolution—at least, not obviously. But in the success of plays like *The Entertainer*, *A Taste of Honey*, or *The Hostage* in the heart of London's theatreland there is evidence not only of a very different style of dramatic writing from that encountered pre-war but of a new spirit among theatre audiences. Indeed, so fast do new names among dramatists become notable enough to inspire critical abuse and journalistic comment—Bolt, Pinter, Mortimer, Arden, Jellicoe, Simpson, Shaffer, and others—that it is hard to keep up with them at this transatlantic distance from England. Yet all the omens are that many of these names will soon be as well known on Broadway as they are on Shaftesbury Avenue and Fleet Street.

Before the war anyone who wanted to cite as long a list as this of young writers for the theatre automatically consulted the *New Yorker*: but, with Arthur Miller silent in the theatre for the past six years, Tennessee Williams remains virtually the only living American dramatist whose name is much in the news outside his own country. After the war the newcomers among dramatists were predominantly French: belated recognition of Anouilh, enthusiasm for Sartre and Camus, praise of a more sober kind and of more modest dimensions for Montherlant and Salacrou, and a hysterical greeting of Beckett and Ionesco. All this occupied some ten years, until, with the London production of *Waiting for Godot* (1955) and John Osborne's *Look Back in Anger* (1956), attention began to shift to England.

Thus, despite the oversimplification latent in any generalization, it is reasonable to take note of an evident shift in dramatic initiative from America in the 'thirties to France in the 'forties and thence to England in the 'fifties. Moreover, it is just as obvious to anyone who has seen or read a substantial number of American and French plays of the years in question that the period of American initiative in the theatre was dominated by an interest in the psychology of the individual, while that of French leadership was as distinctly governed by an interest in philosophy. What both theatres shared in common was an ability to reflect the major interests of the intelligentzia of the time: Freud and Jung (via Strindberg, Ibsen, and O'Neill) set the patterns taken over and developed in American drama, while Schopenhauer, Kirkegaard, and Nietzsche laid the foundations for a drama in France dominated by two men who were themselves professional philosophers. A further influence in France was that of the painters—notably the surrealists—whose concern with the interaction of dream and actuality found its dramatic champions, dimly in Gide and Cocteau, and, more forcefully, in Ionesco. The world of dreams had also figured largely in American plays, but in a more directly autobiographical manner; a tradition in which Tennessee Williams is the direct heir of O'Neill.

All this must be taken into account before it is possible to judge whether anything written in England in the 'fifties can genuinely be described as revolutionary or whether it is in fact no more than a sequence of latter-day reflections of dramatic themes and forms of American and French origin. Is Arnold Wesker, for example, simply our rather belated equivalent of Clifford Odets, or is Pinter no more than the best match we can put up as an answer to Ionesco? Are audiences mistaken in flocking to plays by these and other young authors, who ought rather to be written off as creative artists in the same contemptuous terms as Shaw dismissed Pinero when comparing him with Ibsen? Certainly, compassionate social realism dignified Steinbeck's *Of Mice and Men* or Odets' *Awake and Sing* a good twenty years before English press critics began to commend Wesker's *Roots* on that account or to become phrenetic about Arden's *Live Like Pigs*. Certainly, the nightmare horror that lies between dream world and the actual walked the stage in Cocteau's *Orphé* and Ionesco's *The Lesson* before Pinter wrote *The Room* or Simpson devised *The Hole*. If, then, all that we had to think about in cases like this was a direct comparison of one printed text against another, we might dismiss the new school of English playwrights as derivative plagiarists waking up at overlong last to what the rest of the world knew yesterday. The texts, however, supply only a fraction of the picture. The new style of text is part and parcel of much more general change. Change in the design of building: take a look at the Belgrade, Coventry, or the Mermaid in London: theatres incorporating restaurant, exhibition foyer, and abolishing all vestiges of the class structure of the auditorium that typifies their pre-war predecessors; and similar theatres are on the drawing-board for Nottingham, Leicester, and Chichester. Change in critical evaluation of drama, as exemplified in the advent of *Encore* and *New Theatre Magazine*, two new quarterlies devoted respectively to London and the Provinces. Change in acting style; change in production style; change in design and lighting techniques. Whether it be the repertoire of the Royal Court Theatre, the phenomenon of Peter O'Toole and Albert Finney, Richard Southern's 'Studio' theatre in my own university of Bristol, or Joan Littlewood *toute simple*, the measure of change may appear small if each is taken in individual isolation: but, taken collectively, this degree of change adds up to a new spirit, a new attitude, national and not simply metropolitan. Disinct foreign influences—Brecht, Betti, O'Neill, or Camus— all have their part in this metamorphosis that is overtaking the British theatre: yet it takes more than that to account for the degree of change that I have tried to outline. To explain this we must look for something indigenous; and in seeking it I am persuaded that we must try to put a finger on what in the past should have delayed these changes during the years before the war yet brought them to the fore in the 'fifties.

British plays written in the 'twenties and 'thirties did not create much of a stir either in America or on the continent of Europe: our theatre of that time was predominantly bourgeois and frivolous. In London, 'drawing-room' comedies and thrillers were the order of the day, written to suit audiences that still 'dressed' for the theatre and regarded the playbill either as an after-dinner relaxation or as a prelude to late-night revels. And as all audiences are interested in reflections on the stage of their own attitudes and manners in real-life, so this audience was no exception. As the whisky gurgled out of decanters in 'the library' and teacups clinked on 'the terrace', maids, butlers, gardeners, and other specimens of below-stairs society passed before stage-principals and spectators alike as comfortable jokes, barely human, possessed on occasion of a shrewd mother-wit, but more often with minds as clumsy as their feet and incapable of having any problem of their own which others could take seriously.

Subject matter was equally restricted. Psychology was deemed of itself by these audiences to be 'not quite nice', philosophy to be 'too highbrow', and language and aesthetics either 'too arty' or 'too stuffy'; none of them could therefore warrant a place in postprandial entertainment. Thus, in a climate dominated by plays of the *I Killed the Count* or *George and Margaret* order and by musical comedies, foreign plays on serious themes and native experimental drama had to rely on subsidy from the 'Privilege Ticket Register' or eke out a hole-and-corner existence in clubs at a safe distance from the 'down-town' theatres. Even the classics had a thin time of it, the Stratford season being confined literally to the summer months and Miss Baylis's company at the Old Vic being about as off-beat then as the Royal Court is now.

Our theatre of the inter-war years—I mean the commercial theatre—was thus supplied with a drama of remarkable technical competence, ranging from the Aldwych farces through the polished if vicarious offerings of Maugham and Coward to the comparatively painless social commentaries of J. B. Priestley and Emlyn Williams. Yet in retrospect how incorrigibly vacuous and philistine was the sum total of its contribution to our culture! True, there were some heralds of a change to come: Eliot, Auden, Spender, O'Casey, writing verse plays derived from the example of Yeats and Thomas Hardy. Yet, by the majority, these men and their plays were regarded at best as a disturbing nuisance, Bloomsbury Bohemians; ridiculed as 'the lunatic fringe' because they were feared; feared lest given any encouragement they might disturb the pre-Munich calm of political atrophy and mental indolence mirrored in the musicals, drawing-room comedies, and thrillers of the West End stage.

With the war the theatres went dark.

Perhaps this was a good thing for English drama; for at least when it awoke from the traumatic coma enforced by black-out and air-raid sirens it arose in a remarkably vigorous manner and dressed itself in as remarkably different a style. The most conspicuous change in the theatre when activity resumed after the two-year closure was in the appearance of the audience. Where the wearers of black and white bow-ties had sat beside silks, furs, and diamonds, there were now uniforms of all ranks and many nations, and of male and female cut. Many of the wearers had simply changed one form of dress for another more in keeping

6

with the times; but quite as many were newcomers to any theatre and with very different backgrounds, tastes, and outlooks. The latter, being on leave and determined to enjoy themselves by availing themselves of all the entertainment that was going, took a risk on a theatre for the first time in their lives, overcame their fears of its formal etiquette in the matter of booking seats, buying programmes, and being exposed to the view of other people during intervals, and discovered that they enjoyed what they saw and heard. My own most vivid memories of the theatre when on leave at this time are of Sir Donald Wolfit's lunchtime 'Scenes from Shakespeare', of the Sadler's Wells Ballet led by Fonteyn and Helpmann (where I was often glad to stand in order to get in at all), of the two amazing all-star classical repertory companies at the Haymarket and the New Theatre, led respectively by Gielgud and Olivier, and of the caustic *Rise Above It* series of revues. Most of this repertoire I was seeing for the first time, or seeing so well done that I could not hope to see it bettered. And in this I was in the majority among those audiences; for the excitement and enthusiasm which these plays and performances generated, whether in the queues at the box-offices and gallery doors, in the auditoriums, or far away from the theatres in bleak military camps, was in itself something of a portent. When, for example, people who had never found themselves in any theatre (except for the annual Christmas pantomime) could fall to comparing Wolfit's *Lear* with Olivier's, or to discussing Rattigan's *While the Sun Shines* in a bracket with Congreve's *Love For Love*, as a new and fascinating exercise, it was hard to resist the conclusion that the theatre was receiving a blood-transfusion of some consequence to its future. Nor was it only plays and acting which attracted attention: the stage designs of John Piper, Leslie Hurry, and Tanya Moiseiwitsch, and the skill in production of Tyrone Guthrie and his fellows, took a prominent place in such discussions.

At this distance from the event it is easy to recognize the influence of two external factors upon this remarkable change in attitude to the 'legitimate' theatre. The first was the astonishing development of British Ballet, which in a mere thirty years had translated itself from a state of non-existence into the most genuinely popular form of live entertainment in Britain. Attracting to itself a large audience of shop-girls, clerical workers, and others who would never have patronized a theatre of words on their own initiative, the ballet, with its direct sensory appeal to eye and ear and the easily recognizable virtuosity of its leading dancers, gave new life to a concept of theatre that had been dying a swift death since motion pictures took over the spectacle of melodrama and since managements in the commercial theatre had started to transform the 'well-made' play into the 'one-set' play and the 'small-cast' play. From attending performances of the ballet, audiences both recovered an appreciation of theatricality and rediscovered something of the range of emotional possibilities implicit in dramatic art. These factors, familiar enough to audiences in the nineteenth century, had withered and become desiccated in the 'witty' comedies, the neatly tailored thrillers, and the arid moralizing of expressionist plays during the interwar years.

This popular reawakening to the potential of the live theatre in the colour, movement, and sound of ballet—all so far removed from and in such vivid contrast to the grim realities of casualty lists, ration books, and air-raid shelters—was accompanied by an intellectual stimulant no less important. This was the sequence of plays of every conceivable description carried direct into individual homes all over the country by a public service system of sound broadcasting.

Never since Tudor times had so many people the chance to sample plays of such variety and so frequently *for themselves*. I stress 'for themselves' because this service rendered by the drama department of the B.B.C. was the first direct challenge at popular level to the puritan legacy of hostility to the theatre which has so bedevilled British drama for the past three hundred years. For generations the children of the middle classes in England had been brought up to despise and fear the theatre as something, if not positively evil, at least highly dangerous to both morals and respectability. Short of the demon drink, nothing was to be so strictly shunned. The radio in the living-room offered the young a different picture. Night after night, when petrol rationing, the black-out, and the blitz combined to enforce domesticity, entertainment and relaxation were provided by the invisible actors of radio play, radio feature-programme, radio documentary, and comedy half-hour. ITMA, It's-That-Man-Again, Tommy Handley, became a national byword. His puns and his wisecracks revived an interest in word-play and language without parallel in the experience of young and old alike and started a chain-reaction which led *via* parodies of service life at *Much-Binding in the Marsh* and *Waterlog Spa* to the zanies of *Take It From Here* and *The Goon Show*. Features and documentaries brought the more serious side of wartime service experience directly into the lives of the parents and relatives at home and created the taste for the dramatic television journalism of the future represented by programmes like *Panorama* and *Monitor*. 'Saturday-night Playhouse', followed in 1945 by the introduction of 'World Theatre', brought an international repertoire of plays new and old (representing civilizations of many sorts) to a regular audience of some twenty million listeners. To obtain an audience of this size a play in a theatre would normally have to run twice-nightly for some ten years in the largest playhouse in the country. No one who had been subjected over ten years or more of sound broadcasting to so many plays could easily undergo this experience without questioning in some measure the validity of the traditional taboos on plays and theatre-going: and for the young, at any rate, an appetite had been whetted for sampling the genuine article instead of the echo.

It was on this crest of interest and feeling that Eliot and Fry achieved popular successes with a series of verse plays decorated by distinguished casts in the immediate post-war years. Plays like *The Lady's Not For Burning* and *The Cocktail Party* not only succeeded in London but were swiftly given productions in provincial repertory theatres and in foreign countries. Managements, thus encouraged, risked importing a wide range of similarly serious foreign plays, mostly American and French. The boom in Shakespeare and the classics continued to swell: Dryden, Vanbrugh, and Jonson found champions among leading

9

actors and producers. All this, intermingled with the still growing prestige of the ballet, the constant 'ground bass' of good radio-productions, and the resumption of television, together with the unprecedented activities of the Arts Council in subsidizing good work of all description, opened the way to a future of bewildering possibility. Revolution was in the air. Perhaps, therefore, the strangest feature of the revolution when it came in the 'fifties was that it took a direction unlike any of the more obvious sign-posts pointing to its advent. It may be pinpointed in the production of two plays: John Whiting's *Saint's Day* in 1948, and John Osborne's *Look Back in Anger* in 1956.

Both plays received a greeting from the newspaper critics about as encouraging as that accorded Strindberg and Ibsen by Clement Scott and William Winter in London and New York. Perhaps the most notable feature of this critical drubbing was the proof which it offered that something shocking and unfamiliar, even genuinely new, had arrived: and for the remainder of the decade press hostility has continued to provide a rough guide to those plays which represent a sharp break with traditional attitudes or forms. In fairness it must be said that Mr. Hobson recognized in Beckett and in Pinter those qualities which have since come to be widely acknowledged as excitingly adventurous, while Mr. Tynan performed the same service for Mr. Osborne. However, what really turned the tide of public opinion in favour of the revolutionaries was not the press at all, but television.

When *Look Back in Anger*, the work of an unknown Notting-ham actor, was tottering between the hostility of press reaction and the indifference of public reaction at the box-office of the Royal Court, one of the newly founded Independent Television Companies (Granada) decided to relay the play and thereby changed the fortunes of both play and author overnight. What-ever the play's shortcomings in normal critical terms of reference, its dialogue struck home to viewers as truer to life as they knew it than anything they had yet heard or seen flow between actors' lips. Within a few days the 'House Full' signs were posted outside the Royal Court: Mr. Osborne and his play became the subject of interviews, magazine articles, and fashionable small-talk. Sir Laurence Olivier boldly offered to add the weight of his name to the young author's if he could write another play with a suitable part for him to act. *The Entertainer* followed and, thanks to Olivier, so did the break-through to the West End.

Opinion will vary for some time to come on the merits and failings of these two plays. Neither of them, in my opinion, warrants comparison with the masterpieces of the past; indeed, it would be as stupid and unfair to make such a comparison as to measure *Henry VI* or *The Two Gentlemen of Verona* with *King Lear* or *Twelfth Night*. Both, however, may properly be regarded as revolutionary plays if only because their performance made it impossible for British dramatists to continue serving up an assortment of pre-war theatrical clichés in place of genuinely human characters and dialogue and *get away with it*. Both plays were at least good enough to become points of reference in their own right, for they were the first to make explicit in the theatre the social revolution which had overtaken British society since the outbreak of war. The Welfare State—or at least a substantial chunk of it—lay exposed to audiences for scrutiny. Gone were the stock figures of the comic servant, the moronic policeman, and the sentimental gardener as the sole representatives of proletarian life: in their place were a number of working-class figures who took themselves and their problems seriously. And in a society which was and remains obsessed with the consequences of social revolution in its daily living, this change in the theatrical mirror could scarcely pass unnoticed in the way that the much larger changes in moral values reflected in John Whiting's plays had gone unnoticed.

Whiting's prize-winning *Saint's Day* had been a nine-days-critical wonder in 1948. *A Penny For A Song* (1951) and *Marching Song* (1954) did not exactly fail—both received distinguished productions from a commercial management —but neither created any sort of stir. *Saint's Day* was an attempt to reflect a whole society on the brink of tearing itself to pieces: by comparison, *Look Back In Anger* and *The Entertainer* treat directly of matters of immediate moment as seen from a particular social viewpoint: and where all Whiting's plays wrestle honestly (if inadequately as yet)* with the major moral problems facing Western society today, Osborne's reflections of the world about him are journalistic by comparison. The leaven of Whiting's work, therefore, while it has been steadily working, is slower in maturing and in manifesting itself than Osborne's.

It is hardly surprising, then, that it should have been Osborne who has had the spate of imitators, and that their work should have come collectively to warrant description as 'the kitchen-sink school'. The impact, however, of Osborne's plays has not been limited to the social-realists among playwrights. It has released a flood-gate of talent suspected by none (or very few) among young people of proletarian background who have chosen to express their views in play-form rather than in novels or in slim books of verse or in political pamphlets. They in their turn have inspired others with more traditional literary backgrounds to put the theatre first rather than last on the list of markets for their work.

The most literal followers of Osborne are Shelagh Delancy and Arnold Wesker, authors respectively of *A Taste of Honey* and *Roots*, to name only those plays which, having found appreciative audiences in the West End of London, are now scheduled for transfer to Broadway.

If Osborne's sharp social and political satire is soft-pedalled by both these authors, they have each added in their respective portraits of industrial slum-life and isolated agricultural community a compassion and an acuteness of observation that is just as telling in the theatre. If in the auditorium one is less aware of the astringent note of protest that is so characteristic of Osborne, one is keenly alert to the pathos implicit in proletarian figures who are either unaware of the opportunities which a social revolution has given to them or who

* *The Devils*, produced recently at the Aldwych Theatre, suggests that revision of this statement has become necessary.

are inhibited by traditional conservatism in their ability to make use of them.

On the evidence of *Live Like Pigs*, one might regard Mr. John Arden as a traveller on the Osborne, Delaney, Wesker waggon: but one would be seriously mistaken. The more recent *Sergeant Musgrave's Dance* and *The Happy Haven* (as well as his play for television, *Soldier, Soldier*) tell a different story and point in a different direction. Here is an author who appears to be as concerned with problems of form as with questions of subject matter; an author ready to use period costume, to experiment with ballad and rhyme, to employ masks and an open stage. At the very least there is as much of Whiting's influence at work in Arden's plays as there is of Osborne's; and time may yet show that Arden has as much of his own to contribute to the revolution as either of them. Society's capacity for self-destruction and its corresponding ability to survive almost despite itself lurks beneath the surface realism of *Live Like Pigs* and declares itself in blatant tones in the later plays: tragically in *Sergeant Musgrave's Dance*, comically in *The Happy Haven*. Tribute to the power of the former was paid by the critic of *The Guardian*, who declared after the first night that had the play been written in German, the author would have been hailed as the new Ibsen, the new Büchner, or the new Brecht; but since it was written in English . . . well!

In his concern with the extraordinary contrasts between the declared intentions of human beings and the actual results, Arden's work has affinities with that of two other young dramatists, N. F. Simpson and Harold Pinter, both of whom are indebted to Kafka, Orwell, and Beckett for much of what they write about and how they present it. Simpson uses the technique of literal interpretation of the figurative in everyday speech to parody actions and processes normally taken for granted and, as in the courtroom scene of *One-Way Pendulum*, does this with such devastating effect as to prove that black is white and vice-versa— as disturbing an experience as it is entertaining. Pinter, too, works in the medium of the verbal cliché. Where, however, Simpson rarely appears to be attempting more than an expansion of a familiar technique of modern radio-comedy into full-dress theatrical terms, Pinter's *The Room* and *The Birthday Party* (and now *The Caretaker*) seek to convey aspects of life which the realistic theatre has hitherto elected to ignore, as much a supra-realism of the theatre as anything which earlier surrealist painters sought to depict on canvas. The distinguishing characteristic of a Pinter play lies in the fact that almost everything of consequence he has to say is to be found between the lines rather than in them.* The effect is both comic and frightening; for one seems to see the minds of characters isolated from their utterances, their thoughts distinct and separate from their words, frequently contradicting one another. It is the intention informing this connection between the words and phrases and the lack of connection in the thoughts underlying the words and phrases which makes the difference between comic and sinister effect. While the characters sit talking one may laugh both at and with them: but as soon as action begins to develop out of the words, one begins to perceive how unreliable language is as an indication of human purpose, conduct, or action. The heart of the jungle-savage beats menacingly near the veneer of civilized manners. It becomes possible, for example, to believe that the many Germans who protested after the war that they knew nothing about the horrors of the concentration-camps in their own countryside were telling the truth: it becomes possible to realize that staff for such camps, given altered circumstances, could be found among Britons and Americans.

Pinter's heroes are about as trivial as characters can be; a far cry from the noisy self-pity of Osborne's Jimmy Porter and Archie Rice or the evangelistic fulminations of Arden's Sergeant Musgrave. But because they happen to be comparatively inarticulate they are no less valid as representatives of twentieth-century democracy. These people are indeed prisoners of bureaucracy and the voiceless victims of the tyrant equality.

One swallow, as the proverb goes, does not make a summer; and neither Pinter's recent contributions to the theatre nor those of the other dramatists I have mentioned may add up to anything

* Specimens of Pinter's dialogue may be seen on pp. 26–28.

of revolutionary proportions when judged in isolation. Yet when all of them are thought of in conjunction and their work is looked at in the context of the past five years collectively, it is impossible not to sense a radical change of intellectual and artistic climate. The play of political and social dialectic, deriving from Shaw, Arnold Bennett, and J. B. Priestley, has flowered with fresh vigour and novel attributes of tone and colour. The play of poetic imagination, with roots in Thomas Hardy, Yeats, O'Casey, and the mime-and-dance theatres of oriental countries, has re-emerged with a greatly enlarged audience. And at the same time the pre-war manners-drama of the drawing-room has been transformed into something less frivolous and parochial by Angus Wilson, Robert Bolt, Peter Shaffer, John Mortimer, and Ann Piper. *The Mulberry Bush, Flowing Cherry, Five-Finger Exercise, What Shall We Tell Caroline, The Man-Eaters,* although each is as yet the only evidence of its author's dramatic powers,* suggest corporately that even the middle-of-the-road social drama of today is in far closer touch with the fringes of the experimental art-theatre than it has been for generations. Indeed, on seeing Brendan Behan's *The Hostage,* it becomes impossible to draw any firm line between the two.

It is easy when one has a vested interest in the future of any product to take too lenient or optimistic a view of its respective shortcomings and successes. Beyond all doubt, however, is the vitality of this new theatre of the 'fifties, a vitality moreover that augurs well for the 'sixties. It is discussing in an intelligent fashion almost every major issue of present-day concern: the freedom of the individual within societies where mass conformity is the order of the day, colonialism, the function of the family in modern society, the colour-bar, war, and the H-bomb. It is for the most part a drama of protest, a drama in which the modern tyrannies of apathy, of conformity, and of tolerance of violence are remorselessly exposed and questioned. And on this account it cannot avoid rousing a hornets' nest of shocked, angered, and

* Robert Bolt and John Mortimer have since consolidated their position with other notable plays.

bewildered critics; but by the same token it is winning for itself a large new audience of young people who recognize in this theatre an honest attempt to give expression to their own anxieties, their own aspirations: an attempt which goes by default more often than not in the press, in political addresses, and the other forums where it might normally be expected to figure.

There are two points to add on the debit side.

First, it can be objected that despite the vitality of the subject matter treated in the new drama, there is a singular lack of style relating any one aspect of it to another: some people would go further and say that the notable absence of style in any of it is itself a common characteristic and a dangerous one at that. This, however, is not a matter I can appropriately discuss now, although it is one in which the universities ought to take a much keener interest than they do.* For the moment one may reply, quite fairly I think, that scholars have consistently found that in the historical past variety of style normally accompanies any new literary or artistic development possessing sufficient unity of purpose to be described as a school or movement; also that fusion of a variety of initial styles is a demonstration of the movement at its zenith. I do not myself see the zenith of the modern British theatre and its drama within sighting distance yet.

Secondly, despite the obvious renaissance in interest in the theatre and the changed nature of the plays, theatres continue to close, companies continue to be disbanded, the buildings continue to be pulled down, and the sites continue to be taken over for more remunerative commercial purposes. I suspect, however, that most of the theatres in question deserved this fate. In many instances the buildings were old-fashioned enough to be objectionable to their patrons, shouting class distinction from their entrances and exits, from their sight-lines and upholstery, from their fenced-off galleries and foyers. Others, dingy in appearance, lacking adequate refreshment facilities, ferociously rude at the box-office and ill-equipped with car-parking amenities, had

* This question is discussed in the next chapter.

translated theatre-going from the festive occasion which it formerly was into a form of self-inflicted torture. In others, repertoire, acting, and production were of a standard which television drama could and did put to shame. Why then should any sane person go to the trouble of booking seats, of contending with parking problems and the vicissitudes of English weather, and paying in hard cash for what he could watch and hear, free and in comfort, in his own home? The collapse of the theatre in many provincial cities is due to causes of this kind, and the blame must rest squarely with the *laissez-faire* complacency of the owners and managers. It is hard to prove that any manager has deliberately starved his theatre of the money to keep it clean and attractive in order to be able to sell out at a fat profit to property speculators, and it would probably be unjust to try to do so: but anyone who has watched the progressive deterioration of particular buildings over a substantial period of years and wondered why none of the ticket-money he has contributed regularly to the box-office should have found its way into a restoration or improvement fund is entitled to ask whether such a system of theatre management can possibly serve the new drama to anything but its disadvantage.

It is significant that the new drama has in fact been sponsored, for the most part, by new managements with a very different outlook. They have positively set about finding audiences for their theatres, instead of just assuming audiences will come and then lamenting their apparent reluctance to do so: they have tackled the factories; they have organized playgoers clubs; they have endeavoured to interest children and teenagers. And there are some positive signs that their initiative is commending itself to public opinion. The idea of subsidy is no longer the anathema that it once was, and just as the public has come to recognize the advantages of preserving natural beauty spots and historic monuments as a national amenity financed out of taxation, so there are signs that the public will accept subsidized Arts Centres managed on their behalf by public trusts. Coventry has blazed a trail: others have given notice of intention to follow suit: and locally elected guardians of public funds do not invest sums of £300,000 or more in a dying horse. For the moment, however, a large question mark still hangs over the British theatre. Is there to be a revolution in management and administration to match the revolution in the drama? Or is it going to be another example of the familiar adage, 'too little, too late'? Nor is the question merely one of money. It is one of men and women, of vision and faith, of will and efficiency. And of integrity.

In supplying the answer to this question I think the universities have an important contribution to make. If graduates will not soil their hands or put their trained intelligence to work to this end, then they can have small right to criticize the business men who do. For those of us who study and who teach in universities, the time has come to wake up to the fact that the days when it sufficed to dabble with plays in the dramatic society or even to use that dramatic society as a stepping-stone to an acting career in the theatre have passed: for this in its way has become every bit as futile in the present situation as writing essays and conducting discussions about plays and their authors when all contact with drama as a living art has long since been jettisoned as of no importance.

We have a galaxy of great actors capable between them of giving a more than satisfactory interpretation of every role written for actors to act. We have a rising generation of younger actors and actresses who give every promise of being able to take over from them. We have a formidable array of young dramatists who have already given evidence not only of being able to match the actors but of a capacity to make a contribution to Western thinking which is of interest to people outside England as well as in it. Yet the danger exists that all this may be thrown away for lack of men and women of corresponding calibre in the managerial and administrative offices of our theatres. University students have as much right as other mortals to regard themselves as God's gift to the stage; but if the theatre really means more to them than a means of publicizing their own egos, then clear thinking and energetic action on behalf of the future organization and financial solvency of the theatre ought to concern them more than it has done hitherto. This I submit is the

PLATE 1. Scene from *Goatsong* by Martin Shuttleworth.

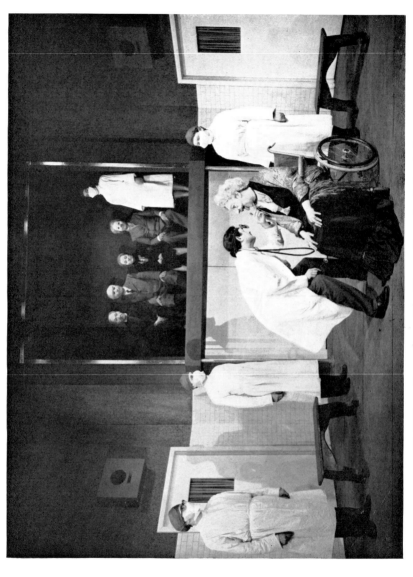

PLATE 2. Scene from *The Happy Haven* by John Arden.

change of heart and of sight-lines that must be accomplished in our universities before they can claim to have played their part in the post-war revolution in the British theatre which, otherwise, is advancing in a most encouraging manner on all fronts.

# II

# Poets and Playmakers*

Aɴ all-too familiar cry from the professional theatre in recent
years has been that of 'Where are the dramatists?' Since
1953 a sustained effort has been made in the University
of Bristol to assist in finding an answer.

In setting out on this quest no one there imagined that the
normal run of undergraduate or postgraduate students could be
miraculously translated by lectures, seminars, practical classes,
and the like, into writers of note. The hard logic of timetables
and noticeboards, however, insisted that the experiment be
labelled; and so, for better or worse, 'Playwriting' has figured as a
subject in the University's curriculum for the past seven years.
This is misleading, since the only regular feature about the class
has been the day and time of holding it: everything else about
the so-called 'Course in Playwriting' has been a variable
quantity from year to year, experiment and expediency playing
a greater part in governing both the subject matter treated
and its actual conduct than formal blue print or obligatory
syllabus.

In effect, these classes have therefore resembled seminars—to
use an academic word—or discussion groups—to borrow a more
popular idiom. On three occasions distinguished Americans

* Judith E. Wilson Lecture in Poetry and Drama, Cambridge University
1960–1.

with sizable experience in the conduct of such classes in trans-Atlantic universities have been imported to take charge of the course. In other years local talent has had to pluck up the courage to conduct the classes. From the start, Aristotle, and such new plays as were being staged in the vicinity, have provided the basic literature of the course: and never has any student been admitted to the course without first promising to contribute a script or scripts for discussion in class. Critical comment on the scripts submitted by other members could confidently be assumed! In other words, Aristotle and new plays provided the tools for critical analysis: original scripts submitted by members of the class provided the subject matter of discussion, analysis, and criticism. And, always, these classes have been held in or adjacent to a theatre with actual production of scripts or parts of scripts as the only test of examination required: I shall have more to say about the vital contribution of the actors later. No degree or diploma is awarded. The reaction of audiences over three nights or sometimes a week of performance is deemed to inform the author more succinctly than any numerical mark what his script is worth: and it is armed with this knowledge that he enters the final post-mortem on his play at which he has to defend his brain-child against the invariably controversial comment of his fellow class members and of the actors, designer, and producer.

What has resulted from this activity? In our rasher moments we are tempted to claim Harold Pinter and John Arden as 'products'. In our saner moments we know that any such claims would, by their falsity, damage—perhaps irreparably—whatever genuine good has resulted from the experiment. Pinter's first play, *The Room*, to which *The Birthday Party* was the immediate sequel, was staged in the Drama Department by chance rather than by careful selection. Both this play and John Arden's farce, *When is a door not a door?* were vetted and approved by the class before the go-ahead for production was given, but neither took its being from the class. *The Happy Haven*, recently presented at the Royal Court Theatre for a limited season, and *Goat Song*, to be presented by the Bristol Old Vic Company at the Theatre Royal later this year, were discussed act by act by the class as they were written; but the respective authors, Mr. Arden and Mr. Shuttleworth, already knew what they were going to write about when they came to their interviews for our Fellowship in Playwriting. More actual changes in the script of *The Happy Haven* were effected in the course of rehearsal by the Bristol Old Vic Company than as a result of class comment. The blunt truth is that Mr. Pinter, Mr. Arden, and Mr. Shuttleworth were writers of outstanding talent who happened, at a particular point in their development as persons and authors, to come in contact with a group of people willing to give them a helping hand.* In short, I am saying that they would have been playwrights with or without the classes in playwriting conducted by the Drama Department of Bristol University.

How then, you may well ask, after such an admission do you defend these classes? In reply I would suggest that the answer, should perhaps not be sought in terms of distinguished individual alumni, but rather in terms of the collective value which the mere atmosphere of such a class bequeaths to all its members and, by extension, to others in the university community with whom its members come in contact. As participants, they share an experience which if not scholarly in the sense understood by the research graduate, is at least studious; and in the course of it they become obliged to test all the misty critical theories and opinions they may nurture about plays against the realities—call them arts or crafts as you will—of the stage in action. No member of the playwriting class, for example, would emerge from it with a script that asked a theatrical management to budget for four characters who could be excised from the play without adding or subtracting an iota from the plot—a mistake which brought the pre-London tour of Miss Shelagh Delaney's *Lion in Love* to an abrupt halt. And it is not a large step from such encounters between art and craft in playwriting to the recognizing of parallels between theory and practice in other aspects both of learning and of life. The poet in every individual participant in

* Mr. Pinter, unlike Mr. Arden and Mr. Shuttleworth, did not hold the Fellowship, and was not a member of the class.

the class is brought to an enforced if unexpected encounter with the playmaker; the would-be playmaker comes face to face with the poet.

Lest this *sententia* appear conveniently obscure I had better elaborate upon it: and to do this I must ask your leave to change the drift of my remarks—if only temporarily. In America last summer (1960) I had the chance to direct three plays—John Webster's *The White Devil* for the State University of Iowa; Harold Pinter's *The Birthday Party* for the Actors' Workshop of San Francisco; and the twelfth-century liturgical music drama, *The Play of Daniel*, for the annual Bach Festival at Carmel, California. This probably comprises the widest range of plays I am ever likely to handle in sequence within so short a compass of time. And simply as such it was a most informative experience: but it also served to correlate many random thoughts about plays and playmakers.

Of the three plays in question, Webster's tragedy is the only one which comes within the normally accepted definition of poetic drama.

'Banisht!'

That single exclamation launches the play at a pitch of emotional intensity both unexampled and unsurpassed. Scene follows scene in verse as compressed in sentiment as it is blinding in its imagery.

'Great men sell sheep, thus, to be cut in pieces
When first they have shorn them bare, and sold
    their fleeces.'

'Nature is very pitiful to whores,
    To give them but few children, yet those children
    Plurality of fathers.'

'Both flowers and weeds spring, when the sun is warm,
    And great men do great good, or else great harm.'

As the play moves from one dark splendour to another it gains emotional momentum from its verse until a pitch is reached

23

where it is not far-fetched to describe the final duet between the
dying Vittoria and Flamineo as a *Liebestod*.

> 'My soul, like to a ship in a black storm,
> Is driven, I know not whither.
>
> Then cast anchor.
> Prosperity doth bewitch men, seeming clear;
> But seas do laugh, shew white, when rocks are near.'

By the time this fearful scene of disintegration is reached—a
scene which cuts off in their prime the last surviving members of
a once large and proud family—Webster's verse has made it
possible for us to glimpse a vision of disintegrating values in
society at large, transcending both family and individual—
nothing less, in short, than the death-throes of religious tyranny, a
*Götterdämmerung* of mediaeval faith and philosophy. Nemesis may
strike down characters deemed wicked and corrupt by the con-
ventional standards of mediaeval spiritual and temporal justice;
but it is those very standards of justice and those who administer
them that are the real victims of this tragedy. As Vittoria and
Flamineo face death, Monticelso, Cardinal and Pope, and
Francesco De Medici, a Duke with murder on his soul, side-step
the holocaust they have prepared for others. They live; but
what they stand for is collapsing, rejected, around them.
The dying Flamineo, in some twenty lines of verse, projects
himself and the audience into the agnostic democracy of modern
times.

> 'We cease to grieve, cease to be fortune's slaves,
> Nay, cease to die by dying. Art thou gone?
> And thou so near the bottom? false report,
> Which says that women vie with the nine Muses,
> For nine tough durable lives! I do not look
> Who went before, nor who shall follow me;
> No, at myself I will begin and end.
> While we look up to heaven, we confound
> Knowledge with Knowledge. . . . . . .
> . . . . . . .                          I have caught

An everlasting cold; I have lost my voice
Most irrecoverably. Farewell, glorious villains.
This busy trade of life appears most vain,
Since rest breeds rest, where all seek pain by pain.
Let no harsh flattering bells resound my knell;
Strike, thunder, and strike loud, to my farewell!'

My object in quoting these lines is simply to illustrate, from a play generally acknowledged to be great, and of which I have recently had first-hand experience on the stage, what I take to be a poet's purpose in the theatre. In producing the play I tried with the actors, with the designer and technicians at my disposal, to interpret the playwright's shorthand of plot, of character, of thought, of language. At the level of appearances we found ourselves faced with a sequence of melodramatic moments, slanging matches, individual tirades, sword-fights; moments of ghoulish horror, pathos, madness, sexual titivation. The plot was complicated, the names and relationships of characters hard to remember—yet in the verse lay first a clue suggesting that as a whole the play amounted to more than this: and, secondly, in the verse there did indeed lie a full and final revelation of the poet's vision, binding all the melodramatic moments into a single coherent pattern. I do not claim that we succeeded in communicating the vision in precise measurable terms to our audiences, but I do claim that by studying the verse we were enabled to recognize the vision ourselves. With that done, we could set out to provide our audiences through the varied arts of the theatre with an emotional experience through which it might be possible for them to grasp something of that vision for themselves. This was poetic drama—the poetry of language, colour, sound, and movement—a world, in short, of emblems, the handmaids to revelation.

Transferring my attention within a week from Webster's *White Devil* to Harold Pinter's *The Birthday Party*, I journeyed in poetic and theatrical terms about as far as there are miles between Iowa City and San Francisco, and that's two thousand. Here is the opening scene of Pinter's play.

MEG: Is that you, Petey? (*Pause*)
    Petey, is that you? (*Pause*)
    Petey?

PETEY: What?

MEG: Is that you?

PETEY: Yes, it's me.

MEG: What? (*Her face appears at hatch*). Are you back?

PETEY: Yes.

MEG: I've got your corn flakes ready. (*She disappears and reappears*)
    Here's your corn flakes.
        (*He rises and takes the plate from her, sits at table, props
        paper, and begins to eat.* MEG *enters by the kitchen door*)
    Are they nice?

PETEY: Very nice.

MEG: I thought they'd be nice. (*She sits at table*)
    You got your paper?

PETEY: Yes.

MEG: Is it good?

PETEY: Not bad.

MEG: What does it say?

PETEY: Nothing much.

MEG: You read me out some nice bits yesterday.

PETEY: Yes, well, I haven't finished this one yet.

MEG: Will you tell me when you come to something good?

PETEY: Yes.

      (*Pause*)

MEG: Have you been working hard this morning?

PETEY: No. Just stacked a few of the old chairs. Cleaned up a bit.

MEG: Is it nice out?

PETEY: Very nice.

    (*Pause*)

MEG: Is Stanley up yet?

PETEY: I don't know. Is he?

MEG: I don't know. I haven't seen him down yet.

PETEY: Well then, he can't be up.

MEG: Haven't you see him down?

PETEY: I've only just come in.

MEG: He must be still asleep.

This play—the first of Pinter's to be presented in America—opened on July 19th. It has now passed its hundredth performance and looks like lasting out the season? Why? What is there about this most English of plays that can account for its becoming a popular success in America?

Apart from one short song there's not a line of verse in the play. The language nevertheless is notably more than just sequences of words. It is both recognizably the language of the characters who speak it—English indeed 'as she is spoken'—and yet a language of remarkable rhythmic and melodic quality, a language which every married couple speak when neither party is really listening to what the other is saying. Here is another passage:

STANLEY: I once gave a concert . . . It was a good one too. They were all there that night. Every single one of them. It was a great success. Yes. A concert. At Lower Edmonton.

There are eight sentences here and only four verbs. At least that is how the speech is punctuated.

STANLEY: I had a unique touch. Absolutely unique. They came up to me. They came up to me and said they were grateful. Champagne we had that night, the lot (*Pause*). My father nearly came down to hear me. Well, I dropped him a card anyway. But I don't think he could make it. No, I—I lost the address, that was it. (*Pause*). Yes. Lower Edmonton.

The cross-rhythms of this language are as delicately sprung as a good dance floor, and take a good actor to do them justice. Or take this:

GOLDBERG: Do you recognize an external force, responsible for you, suffering for you?

STAN: It's late.

GOLDBERG: Late! Late enough! When did you last pray?

MCCANN: He's sweating!

GOLDBERG: Is the number 846 possible or necessary?

STAN: Neither.

GOLDBERG: Wrong! Is the number 846 possible or necessary?

STAN: Both.

GOLDBERG: Wrong! It's necessary but not possible.

STAN: Both.

GOLDBERG: Wrong! Why do you think the number 846 is necessarily possible?

STAN: Must be.

GOLDBERG: Wrong! It's only necessarily necessary! We admit possibility only after we grant necessity. It is possible because necessary but by no means necessary through possibility. The possibility can only be assumed after the proof of necessity.

MCCANN: Right!

GOLDBERG: Right? Of course right! We're right and you're wrong, Webber, all along the line.

MCCANN: All long the line!

Three characters are speaking in this interrogation episode, but the rhythmic structure is a single sequence. The horror of this remarkable scene, and its impact on the audience, is achieved by the deliberate antithesis of verbal *non-sequitur* against the remorselessly mounting insistence of the verbal rhythm. Mr. Pinter may have had little literary training as a dramatist, but as a professional actor he knows better than many trained in letters that an actor's hold upon his audience lies in what he can do with his voice rather than his ability to memorize and speak lines: that it is of greater consequence to an actor to be audible and fluent than to be strictly accurate. His text accordingly gives its actors something of the musical, vocal qualities of *The White Devil*. Despite the seemingly flat prose clichés, the text is theatrically poetic. Moreover, in *The Birthday Party*, by coincidence, there happens to be a parallel between the two interrogators, Goldberg and McCann and Cardinal Monticelso and Francesco de Medici in Webster's *White Devil*. As villains, respectively, of the two plays, both are distinguished by their plausibility and self-esteem. Both stand for Church and State, as well as just being themselves, and both survive the catastrophe of the final dénouement of which they are the arch-contrivers. For this reason, if for no other, I find *The Birthday Party* a play much more profound and genuinely artistic than the simple photograph of a proletarian boarding house that it might seem at first acquaintance. Poet and playmaker are both very much in evidence in this particular sample of the drama of our times.

It is a far cry indeed from this slice-of-seaside-life to *The Play of Daniel* which formed my next assignment in the States. Seven hundred years: no less.

> 'Ad honorem tui, Christe
> Danielis ludus iste,
> In Belva coest inventus
> Et invenit hunc juventus'

Thus it begins: and it ends,

> 'In te Domine speravi: non confundar
> in aeternum.'

It is wholly sung. Or rather it was intended to be. English verse narration has been interpolated in the version prepared for modern performance. Written by W. H. Auden, these plot résumés (for that is their purpose) are hardly inspiring when read in print: but as language to be spoken—more particularly to be spoken after and before singing—it could hardly be bettered. For this verse with its alliteration and strong rhythms enables the narrator to make transition from one sung passage to the next without the bathos that would accompany a strictly literal prose synopsis.

The temptation for the producer of this play is to overlook its extreme simplicity and to impose upon the childlike directness of the story a fussily theatrical presentation. The great lesson to be learnt from the text is that the conflict between protagonist and antagonist—Daniel for the Jews; Balshazzar and Darius for their enemies—is contained within an austerely formal ritual. The dialogue is presented operatically along the lines familiar to us as recitative, aria, duet, quartet, and chorus. Visually this formal vocal structure is matched in the processionals by means of which all characters of importance make their entrances and exits. For the rest, stillness and pattern have as great an importance to the communication of the play's atmosphere and meaning as does the recurring stage direction PAUSE in Pinter's text. Even sense of smell can be important. Both the *Daniel* and *The White Devil* make substantial use of incense.

Having said something of the differences in these three plays, let me now add a personal gloss on two similarities which struck me forcibly when actually working on them.

First, all three are concerned with good and evil at work in the world. Secondly, all three, in what they have to say about it, short-circuit rational discussion of these issues by challenging their audiences to direct, instinctive response to them. Certainly, the story, words, and characters are all simulated with sufficient attention to the detail of actual appearance to make them rationally acceptable to audiences: but it is in the much more elaborate appeal to sensory appreciation that these playmakers endeavour to communicate their understanding of their society and their world to their own and to later generations. If they seek to instruct, they do so by entertaining.

This has been a long digression from the gist of my initial remarks on playwriting classes: but I hope it has helped to make plain what I meant in saying that poet and playmaker meet each other face to face as members of such a class. Moreover, we now possess sufficient common data to pursue a rather closer examination of their respective natures.

To take the poet first. As I learnt from the three productions just discussed, the dramatic poet is in effect a soothsayer, a prognosticator, an individual endowed with power to reveal the agency explaining the relatedness of things—a quality denied to most of us. Yet all of us, independently of one another, observe the phenomena of life, collect and store these observations, filling our minds from floor to ceiling like some vast bric-à-brac shop or auction mart. Most of us spend some time in sorting this lumber in an instinctive endeavour to discover order in it. We stack it in piles. These we first label and then try to relate to one another. The scientist in each of us goes on to examine this relatedness which has been noticed and, whenever possible, to codify it. Effect is related to cause: cause to effect. And so we arrive at a body of knowledge which we label 'experience' and which explains some of this relatedness: but there most of us stop. The professional scientist, of course, will proceed much further. By a process of generalizing outwards from his initial observations of relatedness, his explanations become ever more far-reaching. From so simple an observation as the fact of an apple falling from the branch on which it is growing down to the ground beneath it, he may move in process of time to propelling himself from the ground on which he stands up to the moon and stars above him, simply because he has climbed step by step upwards to an understanding of the relatedness of his own immediate environment to that more distant region of outer space. The scientist is thus truly a man of vision like the dramatic poet: but where his vision is attained by proceeding from below upwards, the dramatic poet's vision, or explanation, runs from above downwards. The poet explains in terms of creative agency. Questions of *Why* and *Wherefore* engage his interest more actively than those of *What* and *How*. In human terms, the doer, rather than the thing done, is for him the object of principal concern. Thus it is the nature of the vision which differentiates the poet from the scientist, and not necessarily the imaginative process of short-circuiting procedures in attaining to it. If, for a moment, I may substitute the word discovery for what I have hitherto called vision, I would say that both poetic and scientific discovery come about as imaginative acts; acts which result either directly from or indirectly within a state of heightened emotional tension. This tension may take the form of emotional excitement or emotional exhaustion. What matters, either way, is that the normal restricting barriers of logical progression or analysis are temporarily lowered or removed. The humility of spirit or the active compassion accompanying this state of mind permits the encounter with truth. That is the moment of discovery or vision.

'Lo, with the ancient
Roots of man's nature
Twines the eternal
    Passion of song

Even Love fans it,
Even Life feeds it,
Time cannot age it,
    Death cannot slay.

Deep in the world-heart
Stand its foundations,
Tangled with all things,
    Twin-made with all.

Nay, what is Nature's
Self, but an endless
Strife towards music,
    Euphony, rhyme?

Trees in their blooming,
Tides in their flowing,
Stars in their circling,
    Tremble with song.

32

God on His throne is
Eldest of poets:
Unto His measures
Moveth the whole.'

What is here termed 'The Passion of Song' is the poet in the
playmaker, the force driving him to explain by revelation the
agency behind relatedness. This is the divine spark or vision in
the poet which enables him to attempt explanation running
from his own glimpse of agency downwards towards the
relatedness of the most common trivia of everyday observed
phenomena.

The degree of his success—and by this I mean the scale of the
descent that he manages to manifest to others together with the
detail of the steps in that descent—reveals the playmaker in the
poet. Wordsworth has put the matter more neatly than I can hope
to do:

'O! many are the poets that are sown
By nature; men endowed with highest gifts,
In vision and the faculty divine,
Yet wanting the accomplishment of verse.'

If we allow ourselves the liberty of interpreting the words
'accomplishment of verse' to stand for craftsmanship, the playmaker's function, as opposed to the dramatic poet's, begins to
become apparent. And in pursuing this aspect of my subject I
would like to ask for the further liberty of borrowing my
terminology from music.

In any play, the actor, as it seems to me, is as essential to the
playmaker as orchestral instruments and instrumentalists to the
composer of music. Subtract actors from your concept of a
play—whether human beings, puppets, or even Gordon Craig's
famous *Ubermarionettes*—and surely the concept collapses.
Reverting to the terminology of music, the instrumentalist here
contains his instrument in his own person—his voice and phy-
siognomy. From this premise one may proceed to think of one
sort of play as a sonata for unaccompanied actors, of another sort
of play as a concerto for actors and theatrical environment; and it

33

is not a far cry from this line of thought to discussing some plays in terms of symphonic structure. If this were to be propounded as a doctrine, I have reason to believe that Cambridge at least would not be lacking in subscribers. It is in proceeding beyond this point, however, that thinking in Cambridge and in my own university of Bristol may well differ.

I myself have become convinced that knowledge or vision— the capacity to explain in any art—is directly related to practice. In other words, the form that any work of art will take is in large measure conditioned by the productive act of creating it. Seven years of experience in a playwriting class have proved to me that playmakers rarely possess a precedent image of their completed play: not as a whole. Rather do they arrive at a knowledge of what they wanted to say in the process of expressing it. Subject matter—a snatch of dialogue overheard, a strange character, a story—excites, stimulates, irritates, and ultimately provokes vision, like a grain of sand producing the oyster's pearl: the vision when it comes is blinding, urgent, clamouring for action: but, for all that, the initial clarity of the vision quickly becomes blurred and vague in outline: it remains personal, not directly communicable to others: only by the physical process of building the play out of or around the vision in terms of one character reacting to others does it become possible for the poet to reach downwards to the detail of relatedness in everyday affairs. Even when he has accomplished this to the best of his rational abilities, there will remain gaps or loose links in the chain of the dramatic action which only the actor will notice: and until these stumbling-blocks within the dialogue have been remedied to the actor's satisfaction, re-creation of character and action, while possibly proceeding at the level of intellectual truth, cannot proceed at the level of emotional truth.* Author, actor, and producer working thus together provide audiences with a schematic whole by which these outsiders to the poet's original vision may themselves ascend to and thus become sharers of it with the poet. The playmaker is clearly secondary to the poet, but only in point of time-factor and

---

* By 'actor' I mean professional actor. Amateur actors lack the technical knowledge and experience to perform this service.

34

Act I

Act II

Act III

PLATE 3. Settings for *The Merger* by Derek Coltman.

A 'Shutter' Scene

A 'Set' Scene

PLATE 4. Restoration Stage.

activity. Unfortunately, we have come to regard this secondary characteristic as secondary in the sense of inferior, even as unimportant. Both in the theatre and in academic circles the playmaker has been left to fend for himself. Vision and craft have been allowed to part company. For the most part the theatre has ignored its duty to train its own playmakers and has relied upon a race of beings known as 'men of letters' to supply this need. Yet, paradoxical as it may seem, those same universities and schools who claim to have given these men their training in letters have turned their backs with consistent disdain on theatres, players, plays, and playmaking. If you think that I am perhaps adopting a rather old-fashioned position in stressing this point, you will grant me none the less, I trust, that the late Judith Wilson's notable benefaction in respect of this lectureship here in Cambridge still bears the hallmark of novelty and singular enterprise upon it.

One result at least of the divorce which has ruled for so long between letters and the theatre is that a notion has grown up that neither players nor playmakers require any training. A gigantic amateurism has come to deputize for the skilled craftsmanship derived from solid apprenticeship, an amateurism moreover which has been given the semblance of professional approval and respectability by Hollywood and television. Commercial exploitation of personality *tout simple* in these quarters has come to rob the actor who learned to master his instrument before he played it in public of popular respect; and it is now busy doing the same thing for the dramatist. Playwriting more often than not has come to resemble what I might call dramatic doodling. Soap operas and similar moral opiates, portraits of abnormal neurotics drawn in clinical detail, arabesques of words and clichés reminiscent of abstract painting, photographic copies of social behaviour patterns, all of these have come to find a place upon professional stages in the disguise of plays. Stories, characters, thoughts or messages, and language *per se*—in themselves no more than contributory components in the art of drama—have each been allowed to usurp the centre stage position hitherto reserved for mighty opposites—the debate or battle between a protagonist and

D                                    35

antagonist—in which the conflicts of society itself are mirrored. Peter Brook in a recent number of *Encore* writes:

'. . . the development of the tradition of naturalism will be towards an ever-greater focus on the person or the people, and an increasing ability to dispense with such props to our interest as story and dialogue . . .'

Fine! Why not forget society altogether, or at least sever those tiresome connections which link us to it? Let's pretend that it doesn't exist. Or, if we can't manage to carry self-deception quite that far, let's dispense with art and everything else that reminds us that we have a responsibility to anyone other than ourselves. Having suppressed cognizance of the first Commandment, to love God, let us suppress the second, to love our neighbour as ourselves. Then, in this social vacuum, we can quickly absolve ourselves from any sense of purpose, of personal guilt or merit; or, come to that, 'such props to our interest as story and dialogue'. The only trouble here for us as playmakers is that we run the risk of losing our audiences too; for they will be so busy doodling in what Mr. Brook calls 'pure behaviour' that they will have no time to bother with our efforts.

Let all of us indulge our whims for intuitive playmaking and put both on a level of everyday behaviour in the street, pub, or coffee bar. But before we do so let all of us who care about the theatre, about the art of drama, be honest enough with ourselves to admit that theatres have been closing because the acting is not good enough and because the plays are not good enough to keep them open. We love to conceal plain truth behind such euphemistic phrases as 'the competition from television', 'frightening production costs', or 'rising overheads': but the fact that audiences will support some theatres to virtual capacity, whether it be Shakespeare in Stratford or Shaw, Lerner, and Loewe at Drury Lane, exposes these laments as the excuses they are. Our theatre is in danger today, not for lack of players, not for lack of plays, but for lack of art in both. I do not deny the presence of young men or young women of vision in our time, nor do I deny the existence of some notable craftsmen: but neither vision nor craftsmanship can of itself produce art. Art presupposes the co-existence of both in the same person; and where so sophisticated a form of art as a regular drama is concerned, both must coexist in high degree.

I believe that the cleavage between the two may be traced in origin to the Puritan attack upon the theatre in the late sixteenth century. Ben Jonson in 1616 edited and published his own plays under the title of *Works*, and in so doing staked a claim for the dramatic poet to be regarded as a man of letters on an equal footing with the theologian, the philosopher, and the historian. He was ridiculed at the time, but lived to win the laureate's crown: moreover he was succeeded as laureate by another dramatist, Sir William Davenant. Jonson, as far as I know, was the first person, at least in print and in a context other than that of Greek and Roman drama, to describe plays as dramatic poetry. Curiously, it is in the dedication of *Volpone* to the universities of Oxford and Cambridge in 1608 that the words occur. He bemoans the fact that so many people are saying that '. . . in *Dramatick*, or (as they terme it) Stage *Poëtry*, nothing but Ribaldry, Profanation, Blasphemy, al Licence of offence to God, and Man, is practisd. I dare not deny a great part of this, and am sorry I dare not. . . .' He goes on to plead exemption for himself; but that could not be the end of the matter. For Jonson was fighting a battle of personal status. Seeing his reputation as scholar and poet endangered by his association with plays and masks, detested by the more Calvinist-minded Protestants in academic circles, he retaliated by seeking to dignify both plays and masks with the status of literature, a venture in which he found himself profoundly embarrassed by his association with Inigo Jones. Nevertheless, the publication of his own plays, followed seven years later by the Shakespeare Folio, both printed on the lines of works of the Greek and Roman dramatists, succeeded in establishing an important pattern for the future. Presented with play texts printed to be read, whether successful on the stage or not, and justified with Prologues, Epilogues, and strings of commendatory verses, posterity can hardly be blamed for coming to think of plays as literature in the first instance and as specimens of theatrical craftsmanship only in the second, if at all. Before Jonson took this action dramatists are occasionally referred to as stage poets, but more usually as playmakers or as makers of interludes: indeed, in official documents they continue to be known as such long after 1608.

It is as *Playmakers* that Sydney describes them in his *Defence of Poetry* and, if I may long-jump the years into our own times, playmaker is still a better descriptive word than dramatic poet by which to describe Mr. Harold Pinter in the context of *The Birthday Party*. In saying this I do not wish to deprive Mr. Pinter of any esteem due to him as a man of poetic vision, as a dramatic artist. I seek simply, in terms of the three plays of which I had experience in America, to blow away the smoke-screen of literary pretensions with which Ben Jonson and his followers clouded the art of playmaking, and out of which the assumption has arisen that from the mere act of writing stories or describing characters in dialogue form a play results. For to this assumption may be attributed in turn the dwindling respect paid by many aspiring dramatists to those abiding conditions of the theatre—the collective presence of the audience and the actors at whose hands audiences receive the play. It is the more interesting to me therefore that the author of *The White Devil*, the most conventionally poetic of the three plays I have instanced, should himself have recognized the limitations attaching to the written text, whether prose or verse, in the theatre—more exactly, his own lack of self-sufficiency.

'The actor', he wrote, 'addes grace to the Poet's labours: for what in the Poet is but ditty, in him is both ditty and music.'

How many dramatists today give so much as a passing thought to the *music* of the words with which they supply their actors? About one in fifty would be my answer, judging from the plays sent me to read. Indeed, where would even Shakespeare be without Mr. Ryland's devoted labours?

Thomas Dekker makes the same point as Webster but in respect of the dramatic spectacle.

'The Poets', he says, 'drawe speaking pictures': but just as forcefully he adds 'the Painters . . . make dumb poesie'.

How often today does the dramatist, in his anxiety to present commercial managements with a small cast list and a single set, pause to consider that audiences bring their eyes with them to the theatre as well as their ears? That glamour has a right to adorn a stage as well as dirt and dustbins? That only when beauty is revealed in squalor are an audience's emotional responses likely to quicken and grow? That squalor for its own sake revolts, then deadens, and finally disinterests? And how often do student playwrights realize without prompting that what takes five minutes or more to *say* can often be *shown* in as many seconds by something which an actor does? Webster, for example, saves some thirty minutes of dialogue-exposition with his dumb shows in *The White Devil*. In short, the music, the colour, and movement of a play's text are just as essential to the full communication of the dramatist's vision to his audience as is the plain meaning of the words spoken in logical sequence from the stage. Nor is it enough for the actor simply to represent, to just *be*, the character. He must be possessed of the physical qualities and the necessary techniques with which to stimulate his audience into accepting the representation as real.

I would suggest that an obsession with pseudo-science has come to lead both actors and dramatists into the blind-alley of dispensing with any serious care for these primarily technical aspects of their art, its music, its colour, its movement, the very means in fact of sensory as opposed to intellectual communication of ideas. It is not to my mind mere coincidence that ballet and musicals alone today command for the theatre large popular audiences: for there not only is the appeal to the senses still direct but the performers also are still obliged to serve a vigorous technical apprenticeship before their managements would dream of allowing them to appear as 'stars' before a paying public.

As I discovered in America, one of the gravest dangers implicit in the so-called 'method' school of acting is its total reliance on *being* at the expense of what Webster calls *ditty* and *music*. If I tell you that *The Play of Daniel* was put on the stage in four days of rehearsal, *The Birthday Party* in four weeks of rehearsal, and *The White Devil* in nearly four months of rehearsal, I not only speak simple factual truth, but point a more important artistic truth. With the *Daniel* I was handling a large cast of professional opera singers and instrumentalists who had learnt their music before starting stage rehearsals. For *The Birthday Party* I was working with a small cast of professional actors. For *The White Devil* I was working with student actors in a university. These huge differences in time factor were here determined not by the respective difficulties of the three texts, but by the time which I as producer had to allot to supplying the performers with technical means to communicate something approaching the playmaker's total vision to our audiences. All that the opera singers needed from me was guidance in *what* to do. They knew how to do it. For *The White Devil* by contrast some students auditioned for exacting roles like Flamineo and the Cardinal with a vocal range of less than one octave, with breath control sufficient to handle no more than half a dozen words inside a phrase, and with bodies so dumped and slumped by constant sitting at school desks and in motor-cars as to be incapable of appearing in doublet and hose without offending an audience. Lest it be imagined that I am here subjecting American university actors to fashionable xenophobia, I would ask how many of the undergraduates who audition for the Marlowe, the O.U.D.S., or the Dramatic Societies at Bristol and elsewhere, pause to think before they do so what acting accomplishments they possess beyond a desire to be seen as Lear and Cleopatra? When I auditioned to act in a production of *Hamlet* for the O.U.D.S. in 1941 I asked no such questions of myself. I regret to say that although I remember being pleased to learn that the producer had given me the title-part, I do not recollect being in any way surprised. This attitude, in which an assumption of automatic eligibility eclipses the humility of approach that still characterizes the opera singer or concert instrumentalist, is I think just as frequent among would-be dramatists today as it is among actors. And it is here, as I believe, that a university can help. It cannot guarantee the theatre its play-wrights of tomorrow, but it can re-establish an atmosphere or artistic criticism in which the poet's function and the playmaker's craftsmanship can be re-evaluated in their relationship to one another. And if the while we remember that Shakespeare was no graduate, we can equally well recall that without the thinking, the theorizing, and the practice of drama in the universities of the Middle Ages and the Renaissance our English theatre of Eliza-bethan and Jacobean times could hardly have become the wonder of the world it is today.

I am myself delighted to see the freshness of observation which young dramatists like Miss Delaney and Mr. Osborne have brought into the theatre. But I am convinced that without the de-termination to bring an equal freshness of approach to questions of form, as Mr. Arden is attempting to do, freshness of observation *per se* will only continue to lose the theatre those audiences it still possesses. For why pay to see in a theatre a rehash of what you can see for nothing in a bus-queue or a station waiting-room or coffee bar? This is no plea for the slavish imitation of old forms, of the 'dumb poesie' of yesterday, of the 'ditty' and 'music' of an archaic diction—but for a study of form in a context of practical experiment and discussion based on work rather than essays or lectures about work. Questions can be asked in such a class—asked of life itself—and how to mirror them in art. New ques-tions—not the stale old questions, so hackneyed that dons have difficulty in ringing any further changes on them—questions so dull and pedantic that students find it hard to muster any spirit in answering them more virile than a vague tolerance appropriate to a game. The questions raised in a playwriting class relate, where the poet is concerned, to life as it is lived by people outside the university as well as in it: where the playmaker is concerned, the questions raised relate to artistic precept, past, present, and future. Looking back on the past ceases to be an exercise in itself, for the value of the past is here to shed light upon the future, the play in the making—or, as a scientist might phrase it, from obser-vation of the phenomena to open the way to something 'emer-gent'. In making this plea for a measure of professionalism I realize I am committing what is perhaps the only unforgivable sin in a society whose commitment to the amateur is absolute. Yet in urging that this is a proper service for a university to offer to its students today, I can hardly claim to be initiating anything original; for there is precedent from Athens itself. If Aristotle is still worth reading, his example is possibly still worth imitating.

# III

# *Drama in a World of Science**

## I

I T is normal to start an inaugural address with some appraisal of a predecessor's achievements and to give some indication of the change of appearance that a new broom may bring in the dustier corners of the house.

Yet this occasion differs from what is normal in two ways. There is neither predecessor nor precedent—at least in a British context. It would be singularly inappropriate however to let the occasion pass without using the opportunity it provides to put upon record the debt which the department of drama in the University of Bristol owes to those men of pioneer interest, faith, and effort, whose work since the war has led directly to the creation of this first Chair of Drama in any British university.

As a university in which to launch such an experiment, Bristol was singularly fortunate in having Professors Beare and Kitto in charge of its Latin and Greek studies; for their personal interest in drama already enjoyed an international reputation. In this respect the department was scarcely less fortunate in the guidance and help that it received from the present Vice-Chancellor of Southampton University, Mr. Gwilym James, who as Winter-

* An Inaugural Address on appointment to the Chair of Drama in the University of Bristol, 9th February, 1961.

43

stoke Professor of English shouldered most of the administrative burdens of the Drama Department's early years. The contribution of another Vice-Chancellor is so obvious as hardly to warrant mention: however, I think it only right to observe that without the bridge between academic and professional interest in the theatre which Sir Philip Morris has provided as Chairman of the Board of Management of the Bristol Old Vic, as Chairman of the Board of Governors of the Bristol Old Vic School, as a Director of the B.B.C. and as Vice-Chancellor of this university, Manchester would not be going to do tomorrow what Bristol is doing today.

## II

The department has been similarly fortunate in the interest shown towards it by the press. Some might say that it has attracted a quite unwarranted degree of press publicity: others that such notoriety has only been occasioned by the fact that the department was unique. Speaking for myself, I think it is more likely that Bristol, in voting the department into existence, happened to give form and substance to something which in a multitude of vague, unexplored, and unexpressed ways was becoming of interest to people too numerous and too widespread to count except as readers of newspapers. There have been signs—portents, if you like—to support this view. The post-war growth of festivals is one of them: not only the big commercial undertakings—Edinburgh, Aix, Venice, Cannes, Salzburg—but student festivals, both national and international. Another is the number and range of plays that people have encountered for themselves, thanks to a public service system of broadcasting in this country. One municipality, Coventry, has gone so far as to take full financial responsibility for building and maintaining a theatre on behalf of its citizens; and Nottingham is about to follow suit. Other theatres, for the first time in living memory, enjoy limited subsidy from the Exchequer *via* the Arts Council. Perhaps most important of all, the whole English theatre is once again permitted to speak its mind freely on any subject it cares to handle;

four hundred years of religious bigotry and political prejudice as represented in the censorship of the stage imposed by the governments of the first Queen Elizabeth have been at last rolled away by those of the second Elizabeth; and already no other country in the world can boast as formidable an array of notable young writers for the stage as England at this moment—two of them, happily, associated with this place.

Bearing this in mind, it is in the order of things rather than surprising that drama should have reacquired a measure of respectability in academic life. Yet it is ever at moments like this, when struggle encounters a temporary success, that celebration can become the bride of complaisance. In the thirteen years of teaching experience that lie behind us, my colleagues and I have had time and opportunity to conduct a thorough exploration of the subject in the manner of a geographical survey. A first viewing of the terrain revealed a landscape dominated by lofty peaks— Sophocles, Shakespeare, Schiller, or Strindberg (to take only those with sibilant affinities). Yet it was objected to us that these features were under close enough survey already in departments of language and literature for our attention to be redundant. We switched our attention from plays and dramatists to places of performance, to the great theatres of antiquity with their perfect sight-lines and astonishing acoustics—Epidaurus, Aspendus, Orange—to the charm and elegance of theatres in the baroque style—Bayreuth, Schönbrunn, Drottningholm, our own Theatre Royal—or to the intricate complexities of the modern opera house. And again it was objected that these matters were already taken care of by archaeologists and architects. We turned our gaze to stage machines and scenery, to perspective settings, and to the varied possibilities of lighting them by candle, by limelight, or by electricity, and so to the further optical developments that led to the filming and televising of the acted play; only to be advised that such matters lay within the preserves of science. Experiments in acting and other practical activities of the theatre brought protests that such work was better conducted by artists and craftsmen in a vocationally slanted academy than within the contemplative atmosphere of university studies. There remained

45

the study of audiences. What persuaded them to support the theatre at the box-office, to champion its survival against the attacks of its detractors, to prefer one dramatist to another, and to accord actors at one and the same time the status of royalty and near-criminals? Yet these preoccupations, we were told, were not ours either, but those of the economists and social historians, the psychologists and psychiatrists. Drama, in short, was not a subject: simply a collection of fragments, more or less interesting, and all peripheral to sounder disciplines already in existence. And here the horse jibbed: for, as Eugene O'Neill once observed, 'dramatists were psychologists—and good ones at that—before psychology was thought of'. Improving upon O'Neill, we noticed that audiences had been patronizing theatres all over the world long before social history and economics became fashionable subjects. Somewhere in all this careful fencing of special preserves and hedging about of proper and improper interests, was something suspiciously timid, parochial, and inbred—something to be challenged as itself wholly improper to a university because a contradiction of its very name, nature, and function. One might as well say that mathematics was no subject because its many aspects were already well enough looked after in a variety of engineering and science disciplines. Here, under our noses where drama was concerned, we were meeting face to face that fragmentation of knowledge, that artificial divorcing of one aspect of a subject from another, implicit in specialization, that division of society against itself that results in anarchy and is known as barbarism. The charge levelled against drama of being 'no subject' had the ominous appearance of being derived from either plain ignorance or from fear lest its admission might do some damage to the fences and hedges erected around the countless precious allotments and ignore the prominent notice, 'Trespassers will be prosecuted'.

It is pleasant to be able to record that in this university the penalty threatened for any infringement of this notice has been more honoured in the breach than the observance. The Drama Department has every reason to be grateful for the number of Joint Schools, the help received both from the Department of

Physics in elementary optics and acoustics, and from lectures in the language departments where foreign drama is concerned, as also from the instruction in practical aspects of the subject provided by the Bristol Old Vic School and Theatre Staff: all of which testifies to the existence in this place of a broadly humane and co-operative spirit. Nevertheless, one important result of admitting drama as a subject in this university has been to focus attention sharply upon the amount of specialization that exists within faculties and upon the barriers which this specialization has created, dividing one department from another and cutting off one faculty from another. I choose to raise this issue because neither of these factors has helped in any way to define the new subject in the manner which ensured that the teaching of it should be to the maximum advantage of its students. Some people will doubtless object that students have no right to expect any consideration beyond being informed that the subject exists, and that they have opportunity to study it. This attitude, however, if acceptable in an age when higher education was a privilege reserved for the very few, is no longer tenable at a time when students, from the age of eleven onwards, are being trained to regard a university education as the factor which determines economic and social status in later life.

Sir Francis Bacon once boasted that all knowledge was his profession; and indeed the range of his mental activities has amazed scientists as well as students of letters ever since. Yet, however much may have been added to the world's stock pile of knowledge in the four hundred years since his birth, few scientists today have any knowledge of how to prevent the fruits of specifically scientific discoveries being used to plunge mankind into an unparalleled chaos of suffering, destruction, and new-barbarism. Even fewer arts graduates know enough about the modern scientific subjects or processes to which they owe their present standard of living to be trusted with responsibility for the peaceable government of mankind in a world where the individual has committed the control of his agricultural and industrial economy, of his communications, and even of his bodily and mental health, to scientists. In this world of science and

47

related technology the right hand has effectively ceased to know what the left hand is doing—the world in fact of Mr. Harold Pinter's plays or Eugene Ionesco's. It is against this background that I have to ask myself what the study of drama offers to prospective students. Of what possible value can it be to them? Is it just another subject to which they must become slaves? Or may it be a subject which can advance them in the art of living and qualify them to lead others in that art? In our concern for the sanctity of our respective specialities, are we to continue to ignore, with fastidious politeness, almost every issue of serious consequence to the student, from the future of television and the Commonwealth to Africa and the H-Bomb, and rest satisfied with giving him a gilt-edged ticket to present to the Labour Exchange? Is drama to be another special subject of special interest to the special few, or can it cater simultaneously for the genuine specialist enquirer, and for those who are not yet equipped to do more than acquire a general cultural background but form an increasingly large proportion of university entrants? The demands of specialization in arts subjects already impose upon the sixth-form pupil as well as upon the undergraduate fantastically congested lecture time-tables and reading lists. While these demands themselves narrow his mental horizons, they also eliminate the possibility of effective counterbalance, since the student is given neither time for, nor direction in, any studies, humane or scientific, other than his own speciality. Thus instead of preparing himself to understand his own society, its traditions and its prospects, he is systematically isolated from it, insidiously dragooned into becoming, as a graduate, part of a governing class, whose background he does not fully understand or necessarily approve, and cut off from that larger part of society whose dreams and struggles propelled him into the university in the first place. Disappointment, bewilderment, and frustration are the products, and 'Lucky Jim' the representative.

Can drama in the undergraduate curriculum offer us more than this? If not, then I believe we are wasting time and money in admitting it to our prospectus. It would be pleasant to be able to state that in seeking the answer, guidance was forthcoming from the example of other subjects: but it is not. For even where evidence exists of one arts discipline endeavouring to understand and assist its neighbour (as in the many Joint Schools in this university), in general, the right hand of arts subjects, far from being concerned to understand what the left hand of science is doing, often appears to have no deeper interest in its gestures than that of a brother who seeks to prevent a sister from obtaining two sweets when he has only one. Up to the present time drama has simply copied the other disciplines in arts and science in advertising in the faculty prospectus a number of obligatory courses, a number of books for prescribed reading, and a number of obligatory examinations. And in doing this it has been our aim to show the outside world that the subject was as respectable as its neighbours. In this objective I think we can fairly claim to have been successful. But is this to be the end of the matter? Are we to be satisfied with a replica of something which most of us agree to be inadequate and out of date? Complaints, according to *The Times*, have recently come from Edinburgh that 'lectures in some departments are little more than versions of a textbook'. At Birmingham a student told a correspondent of the same newspaper: 'I have been completely disillusioned about what a university is since I came here: I thought it would be doing so many things on such a high plane. Instead I found myself on a course which was so technical and so extensive that all the people in the department were completely wrapped up in their own subject.' Some adventurous undergraduates at Oxford have recently focused public attention on these matters by rather unorthodox and perhaps unfortunate methods; but it is hard to refrain from the comment 'not before time'. I can well remember being compelled myself to attend a course of lectures on bibliography and thinking that this measure of obligation must portend something more than usually worth while—only to be told at the start of the first lecture that 'a book, may, roughly, be defined, as a gathering of leaves', and treated thereafter to a host of such pedagogical platitudes. Warned in this way that obligatory attendance could as easily camouflage flatulence as revelation, I am aware that incorporation of a subject within a faculty prospectus can just as easily disguise a costly form of escapism as advertise a path to wisdom.

Which is it to be for drama?

## III

Lacking any obvious lead from within the university, the suggestions which I have to make by way of answer cannot but be personal. They are however based upon thoughts which have arisen directly from the experience of teaching the subject and from discovering in the course of that teaching what potential the subject contains for the students who read it.

The most exciting single discovery to have emerged from this thirteen-year survey is the way in which drama can treat of Western civilization as a single homogeneous tradition, not like English literature beginning more than halfway through, not artificially divided on a geographical basis like modern languages, not split in two like the self-contained worlds of modern and ancient history, more fortunate than music in that there is no lack of notation from Greece or Rome, happier than classics in being still alive and practised among us here and everywhere. Continuity is its hall mark, the actor its standard bearer, buildings and designs its baggage train, its comic and its tragic masks the expressions of mankind's encounters with his gods, his concern for his fellow men, and his strictly selfish interest in himself. Like some miraculous chameleon, the history of European drama reflects the alternating humility and arrogance of the human mind in its relations with the supernatural and in its contemplation of itself.

A discovery scarcely less important than this image of continuity within our European heritage, which a study of Western drama offers, is the dawning understanding that dramatic traditions within the Eastern world follow similar patterns of birth, growth, decay, and rebirth to those in the West, having remarkable affinities at many points with our own. And who knows what we in this materialistic and technological age may regain from such contact with a society which, busy as it may be in industrializing itself, has nevertheless preserved a much more humble approach to nature than our own? May not the safeguard to the tyranny of science perhaps lie there? A tyranny as alarming in the hold which it has taken on men's minds, as those of religious bigotry and feudal serfdom which we have at last thrown off.

The third discovery of experience is one which the scientist may well regard as too simple to warrant mention, but which in arts subjects has been forgotten or suppressed—the discipline implicit in practical work. Exercises in the control of voice and body, in the creation of a setting or a costume (design and construction), the attempt to write a play, or a radio or film script (enforcing a close observation of other people) or the struggle to co-ordinate actors and craftsmen (all of them wilful and human) into the coherent pattern of a play in action—these things are not to be written off as so much time mis-spent. It is a remarkable fact that no student reading drama as a subject here has failed in his degree exams because of an over-indulgence in practical work. Some critics have argued that such work encourages a vocational approach, destroying or inhibiting genuinely academic study: others have criticized a practice which, by seeking to inform rather than to qualify, serves only to elevate what is amateur and esoteric at the expense of what is professional and realistic. That both such risks exist is undeniable; but in raising such objections both types of critics are overlooking a certain good in their concern for a risk of evil. What matters is that within an arts discipline the hands can be reunited with the heart and with the head: the whole human personality working as a co-ordinated entity. It is no coincidence that modern psychiatry has discovered a therapeutic value in dramatic activity. All drama, Western and Oriental, African and Latin-American, has sprung spontaneously from the fears and joys of the heart; it has been modified, adapted, formalized into religious rituals and civilized by varied forms or genres imposed upon it by the intellect; yet always it has been practised by the speaking, singing, dancing, gesticulating, informed, disciplined, and co-ordinated body. And I refuse to believe that any student today is the worse for having experienced life fully through his mind, his emotions, and his body, even when temporarily confined within a university.

These then are the contributions which drama as a subject can make to the life of a university. It can present the past to its students as a single living and continuous whole. In the present it provides a means of investigating the links connecting Western civilization with that of the East. And in its creative aspects it links past and present to the future. In short, it can provide a forum for the examination and discussion of the human condition, its relationship with its gods, and its interest in itself, collectively and individually, as revealed in its social values.

Arts departments in this country have for the most part dispensed with creative ability. They have relied upon an emotional interest or intellectual curiosity in the student serving as a magnet to attract him to the subject, and have then directed all their attention (once the student is their captive) upon disciplining his intellect within the confines of the subject with an almost total disregard for the emotional and creative aspects of his personality. These have been left to find a fitful outlet in extra-curricular activities to which we pay lip-service when exhorting students to lead a full life in the Union or Hall of Residence and frown upon whenever we meet together to discuss his academic progress. The result is to be seen in a welter of analytical criticism which is predominantly destructive, and in the apathy, the indifference, the complacency, and downright dullness of so much of university life. I would go further and say that our students, in comparison with American students, whatever their respective intellectual attainments, are frequently made to seem emotionally immature and often painfully gauche.

Science and engineering subjects, by contrast, however much we in arts departments may deride their vocational nature, at least make some provision for their students' creative capacities and interests. We are on safer ground if we complain that the scientist or engineer in his concern with man's material environment is dangerously careless in his lack of concern for man's human condition.

Either way, however, it is clear that arts and sciences no

longer make the same assumptions about their students nor the same demands of them: to that extent, therefore, they no longer talk the same language. And if we who teach in a university do not share a common approach to what we are supposed to be doing, how can we expect our students, as graduates in responsible positions, to talk a common language in respect of the world and its government? The example of division, of bickering, and of shut doors which we set them, they carry into life.

It is here precisely that I would commend the wisdom of those men who admitted drama as a subject into this university, for I believe that it has something of value to offer to both arts and sciences. Knowing no frontiers in time past and no boundaries of nationality or creed, it offers a microcosmic image of human purpose and attainment in a form that is convenient to study. For arts, in particular, it not only widens horizons which have become narrow through the constant pressure of specialization, but introduces an element of practical and creative craftsmanship which at present is the prerogative of the science student in his lab, or left to the vagaries of chance in the Union. To science it offers the easiest of paths into the realm of other arts subjects which, if not much frequented by a student while he is struggling against the clock of his degree timetables, has at least been opened up for him to explore later in life when leisure is available. To one and all, arts man, scientist, graduate-duke, and non-graduate-dustman, it offers a forum for the study and discussion of moral values—one of the few surviving forums left to us where the duke's interest and the dustman's can be discussed, not individually and separately, but as mutually related within the framework of society—a commonweal, national and international. Any lingering tendency for the auditoriums of theatres to be respecters of persons is now offset by television. In former times theology was reputed Queen of the Sciences on this account. It was within these terms of reference that Marlowe and many another Elizabethan thought philosophy divine. Today, for better or worse, scientific knowledge has given us a world where what is single and unified in nature has been arbitrarily split asunder, and where the contrasts implicit in nature have been virtually eliminated. The electric-light switch abolishes the distinction between day and night. The sharp contrast of town and country disappears daily in the creeping sameness of suburban sprawl. And in countless homes the binding power of human feeling is either spread thinly on causes remote enough to be only vaguely understood—famine relief in the Congo, flood victims in China, the R.S.P.C.A.—or else it is concentrated upon such microscopic social units as the family circle or the immediate and often wholly selfish wants of the individual. It is not that we as individuals have lost our capacity for interest in moral values, but that the complexity of the life made available to us by a hundred years of applied science and exacerbated by the confusion of two world wars has eroded our sense of corporate responsibility with nature, to a point where each individual is in danger of abdicating it to some mythical person or organization other than himself: having forgotten how to love God, there are many signs that we are also forgetting how to love our neighbour. And this has ever been the acid test of disintegration and degeneracy within a society. It also happens to be something upon which drama focuses attention: for when all is said and done, dramatic art is not plays, not theatres, not scenery, but actors and audiences—a living, vital, communal relationship—there to mirror for society, and all the individuals who together compose that society, mankind's relationships with his gods and with his fellow men at that particular point in time. Great drama is the product of greatness in a people—a concern for God, for society, and for the individual, as acutely mirrored on the stage as it is reflected in the auditorium. Shakespeare could discuss government and politics in his histories, love and its mysteries in his comedies, and the consequences of darker human passions in his tragedies: and he could do this not only with his aristocratic patrons but with the rankest of stinkards, the fellows with grounded judgements and no formal education, who paid their penny to stand in the yard. The Globe stage and auditorium was Elizabethan England in miniature, just as the Theatre of Dionysus was Athens. In the same way the Colosseum provides a faithful reflection of the values by which Rome lived in the imperial epoch; itself a breathtaking feat of engineering science, the spectacles presented in it nevertheless reflecting as accurately the reason for Rome's fall. I hardly need to stress the comparison that could be made with the modern miracles of cinema and television and the uses to which they have been put.

The playwright Robert Bolt has stated the matter in another way and in words notable enough to be worth quoting.

'The Deluge, being an Act of God, threw little light on human nature. . . . An atomic war would be an act of Man, and if, as seems probable, Man destroys himself, it will be because, on balance, Man prefers to; because his hatred of life is stronger than his love of life, because his greed, aggression and fear are stronger than his self-denial, charity and courage. Because, in short, of his nature.

I am aware that the question of Man's nature is an old one, that has been moving up on Man ever since the Renaissance when Man began to move away from God. But because the bomb enables Man for the first time to realize irreversibly whatever fantasies of evil he may have, we . . . are the first generation which cannot dodge the question . . .'

This mirror of moral values in society—of man's interest in himself, of his regard for his neighbour, and of his respect for his gods—is the quintessence of drama as an academic subject: for it is this balance between the three (or lack of balance) in any society which distinguishes one civilization from another. It is the particular quality and purpose of dramatic art to reflect it. Berthold Brecht puts the point in the simplest possible way in a poem addressed to an actor.

'Do not step too far
From the everyday theatre,
The theatre whose stage is the street.
Look—the man at the corner re-enacting
The accident.
Thus he gives the driver at his wheel
To the crowd for trial.
Thus the victim, who seems old.
Of each he only gives so much
That the accident be understood.
Yet each lives before your eyes
And each he presents in a manner

To suggest the accident avoidable.
So the event is understood
And yet can still astound,
For the moves of both could have been different.
Now he shows how both could have moved
To circumvent the accident.
This witness is free from superstition.
Never to the stars
Does he abandon his mortals
But only to their own mistakes.'

This, I submit, is important enough to suggest Joint Schools of the future in partnership with theology, philosophy, history. Bridges moreover exist within the subject of anthropology, to medical psychology, to archaeology, to music, to the fine arts, and of course to literature and languages. The growth of perspective scenery, founded on geometry and optics, and culminating in cinema and television (with all that involves in terms of electricity and the related techniques of sound broadcasting) provides similar bridges to science and engineering subjects.

In short, I ask you to think of drama as a discipline centred upon the comparison of moral values—theological, social, and individual—and equipped at its frontiers with launching sites for a great variety of journeys into other disciplines. Drama, I submit, far from being 'no subject', is in fact a subject with remarkable integrating power, a subject which can relate the ancient world to the present day, which can bring critical appraisal into direct contact with creative experiment, which can provide the arts man with a lively introduction to scientific thinking and the scientist with as lively a reflection of his own human condition. It is this integrating characteristic of drama as a subject which I am anxious to explore and develop in the service of the university and its students over the next few years.

Any discussion of future plans and prospects however at once raises the spectre of numbers: for no planning today can be deemed remotely realistic that does not take into account the revolution, scientific and social, which is obliging us to build new universities and to expand those already in existence. Any planning which ignores these pressures has about as much chance of fulfilment as has the child's sandcastle on the beach of withstanding the incoming tide.

## IV

How many students will be seeking admission? The pressure towards a vast expansion of numbers is already with us. To what purpose? Are all of them likely to gain automatically from subjection to specialist studies? What are these legions of prospective students seeking admission for? An easy answer would be, 'to remove the social stigma of being excluded'. In America this is already true. I suspect that it explains much of the pressure here as well: for it is already clear that many schoolteachers and parents are more interested in the paper qualifications bestowed on a student by a university degree than in what the student is going to get out of the subject he is committed to studying during the most vivid years of his life. One of many particular examples must suffice for illustration of these pressures in action. A student who recently applied for and was awarded a place in one of our special schools showed a degree of personal initiative on arrival by asking to transfer to General Honours in order to be able to read two subjects which interested him and which were not offered at school. The university complied with his wish; but his headmaster intervened, telling him to desist, since as a prospective teacher he could not hope to qualify for an ultimate headmastership himself if he did not graduate with Special Honours. He did what his headmaster told him he must do: not what his heart and head suggested and the university permitted. This state of affairs is with us and is a fact to be reckoned with before we acquiesce in accepting still larger numbers. Surely it is pointless to try to make specialist scholars out of students who have neither the personal enthusiasm for the subject nor the academic capacity required to become scholars in any genuine sense of that word. Yet that is exactly what we are already doing in allowing our numbers to increase year by year without making any equivalent adjustments either in what we offer or how we teach it. We adopt a take-it-or-leave-it attitude in respect of our own specialities, and express ourselves as unconcerned if the number of First Class Degrees remains constant while IIb's, Thirds, and Passes swell in proportion to the increased numbers. Our unconcern, however, does not find a matching response among the students —not at any rate when they discover how much lower is the actual market value of an Arts IIb or Pass than that which their parents or their mentors have led them to expect of any university degree. Where the science student knows that, irrespective of the class of honours gained, he has ten jobs to choose from, the arts man finds that he is competing with ten others for every job that's open to him. In many cases, for all the so-called training of his intellect, he cannot hope to earn as much as his home-town neighbour who works only with his hands. This in itself is not serious; but it becomes serious when his fellow student with a Ist or IIa is challenged by the manual labourer to explain how his Special Honours degree has equipped him to hold managerial office, and neither of them knows the answer. And still we are asked by people whose arts degrees have put them in relevant positions of power in the Treasury, and the Ministry of Education, to make as many new places available in the arts departments as in the sciences. Would it not be as well, before this rat-race of competition with or against the sciences gets completely out of hand, to try to set our own house in order and rationalize our prospectuses to the point where they have a closer resemblance to the needs of the twentieth century than to those of the eighteenth? The Industrial Revolution is, after all, behind us and not ahead.

Increased numbers we must accept because we are part of twentieth-century democracy: this is a social pressure, a product of social revolution and, since most of us earn our keep at the taxpayer's expense, one which we must respect. But can we not also accept the lessons of our own experience and readjust our prospectuses to meet the change? It would be as well if we could: for it is by no means impossible that the taxpayer may insist on auditing our accounts and force change upon us. His refusal to subsidize the arts because he fails to understand that they have a use is familiar enough already; and he could easily apply the same reasoning to most arts subjects in a university. It would be tragic folly to sacrifice this obvious priority to the immediate pressure of larger admission quotas.

This is not just a convenient excuse for side-stepping the problem: rather is it a first step to meeting it. For, given a better understanding of how the subject can help to meet the educational needs of society at the present time, it should not be difficult to arrange the teaching of it in a manner which serves both students and subject. If we can achieve that first, expansion of numbers can follow without risk of staff, subject, and students setting sail in a sieve. I would ask, therefore, for a five-year breathing space before the Drama Department is required to assist in any general expansion of numbers. After that, we must take our share; but when the time comes I would still ask for the award of places to be based only upon a genuine and urgent need, and *not* simply to preserve the balance between places in arts and science faculties. What, in any case, does this word 'balance' mean in this context? If it means encouraging the division of adult society into two halves, neither of which understands or respects the viewpoint of the other, I see more harm than good in this balance. If it means providing society with a surplus of one sort of person whom society cannot easily accommodate while persistently falling short in the urgent demand for another sort of person, I would again question the desirability of maintaining this precious balance. Nor is 'balance' the only word in our academic vocabulary which I would question. We talk incessantly, like characters in an N. F. Simpson play, of keeping our subjects free from the taint of vocationalism, of not lowering standards, of the need for more and more research and of funds to pursue it, without pausing to consider whether such words and phrases have any meaning outside our own charmed circle. In one breath we in arts speak of scientists and engineers as if they were not quite respectable academically because their subjects appear to be so vocationally slanted, while with the next breath we pilfer their research procedures and try to dignify our own subjects with a spurious methodology. But having done this, instead of then applying these methods to the extension of human knowledge and potential, we direct them in ever-narrowing circles to matters of such miniscular public concern that no publisher would look at them. While we in arts potter among these hedgerows picking the modest violets of knowledge, we cannot complain if scientists take all the prizes in the Monte Carlo Rally. Such leisurely picnics in the quiet backwaters of the past are all too tempting, for they absolve us the while from concern with the present and the future. The danger is that we may come to forget what our students expect of us. It is perhaps worth recollecting that when the monastic scholasticism of the Middle Ages lost touch with the society it was supposed to serve, society dissolved the monasteries. I am not arguing that this was necessarily a wise thing for society to have done; but as a warning of the way in which society behaves it is worth recalling. Scholarship is surely the point where the past meets the present: creation the point where the present meets the future. If it is the scientist who these days seems to carry off most of the prizes, and enjoys an enviable self-confidence, whether in gown or town, that, more often than not, is because his work so frequently makes him one of the creators. If the arts man lacks this self-confidence it is often because he has lost track of the present in the desert sands of the past, failing to create anything, failing often even to link the past to the present and attain the distinction of scholarship. It was with a sneaking sympathy, therefore, that I read of the arts graduate who presented a prospective employer with the simple testimonial, 'I have survived an arts degree.'

Too many undergraduates reading arts subjects get hold of the idea, either at school or from us, that the purpose of their studies is to obtain encyclopaedic knowledge of their subject from books and lectures. Yet such knowledge is only scholarship of the third rank, if it be scholarship at all; for it demands no more than an exhaustive command of fact and figure together with the capacity to regurgitate them in condensed form—in short, a discipline of memory. It leaves out of account the ability to relate this knowledge to matters of current moment, let alone the future. Too many post-graduates are already engaged in work with a funereal air about it. Ashes to ashes and dust to dust. I have myself stumbled upon a stack room in a library, far distant from this place, chock-a-block with Masters' theses and Doctoral dissertations neatly sorted row upon row like cremation urns, and all with the same epitaph: 'I have my doctorate. Let my subject rest in peace.'

It is often argued that what matters here is the humanizing effect of the analytical discipline involved rather than the product of the study: but I would beg leave to question whether this follows as axiomatically as is supposed. Retrospection for its own sake—if pursued exclusively—is restrictive and inhibiting. It ignores the fact that the research worker is himself the fire of the present and the spark of the future, and that the creative element within him can wither and die if left to starve. *The Tinker* may not have been a very good play, but what it was struggling to say is important. It asked us to examine our conscience in respect of the 'unsatisfactory student'. Are we sure when we elect to send him down that the failure is *always* in him and *never* in us? Are we always sure that our own preoccupation with the past has not betrayed us into ignoring the factors of the present and the future which count for so much to him? And if—like Jimmy Porter and his angry disciples—he chooses to write off both us and the dead wood of the past as so much time wasted, is he always wrong? It would be as well if we knew the answers to these questions before we glibly decide to double and treble our own numbers for no better reason than to prevent these places being awarded to scientists. Speaking for myself, I would much prefer a small number of genuine enthusiasts to a large empire of listless drones. The time and resources thus saved could then be placed at the disposal of the scientists and engineers to some real effect.

## V

If the problem of numbers complicates any plans for the future, so, where drama is concerned, does the theatre's future as a living art. Drama has acquired a long enough and a distinguished enough history behind it to be recognizable in the twentieth century as an academic subject in Sweden, Germany, Austria, Belgium, Italy, the United States, and now in Britain: but it behoves us at the same time to remember that it always was and still is a living art. Yet we live in a time when theatre companies, along with orchestras, have become the victims of chronic financial anaemia. If we believe in the past, therefore, is it not time we began to practise what we teach? Whether we like it or not, whether we are aware of it or not, the Church and the aristocratic layman have handed the torch of patronage to us. Responsibility for the care of the artistic heritage of the past and for there being any art of the future has passed to the universities. The private patron has died with the past: industry is often a generous and well-intentioned successor, but cannot be expected to have the knowledge available within a university. Gone is the time when it sufficed to note the colour of Maecenas' gown and criticize its texture. Now we have to wear it.

This is a problem which Americans and peoples of the Commonwealth have already had to face in a much more acute form than we have: and if, as I believe, they have found an answer, then we should at least be humble enough to consider it while we still have time. I refer to the admission of practising artists (with or without degrees themselves) to the lawns and classrooms of the campus. They do not come as outsiders to deliver a single lecture and dash away again, but live there and are available to answer students' questions—not in that nightmare five minutes after a lecture, but day in day out—whenever the need is felt. Painters in residence, composers in residence, printers, singers, actors, writers. Results vary enormously. The principle itself is still debated. Many academic people object that the strong vocational element within these subjects creates a pressure towards an undesirable vocationalism in other subjects. Many professional critics outside the universities object that these activities encourage a vast amateurism at the expense of professional standards. Where drama is concerned I would agree.* Nevertheless, but for the universities and schools, America today would be without a theatre—every actor, writer, and designer of distinction being

* This important question is treated at length in the next chapter.

university trained. I would add further that almost every innovation of importance in the whole long history of European theatre has been made by highly educated amateurs. The professional theatre can hardly describe itself as in the pink of condition at the moment, and maybe the moment has come for another shot in the arm from the amateurs. If so, why not from the universities? In my view the duty of the universities to drama as a living art today should be to provide generous and tolerant patronage for critical thinking about the theatre and creative experiment in it. Attempts to do more than that carry with them grave risks of vulgarizing the university and debasing theatrical art.

What is already quite clear in America is that a student society which learns to accept creative artists in its midst as part of a normal landscape instead of as strangers, as frightening outsiders from another planet, is in a far better position to find a use for art and artists in its maturity than are our arts faculties in Britain, where both the fine and the practical arts are still relegated in most universities either to the extremist limits of the timetable or to the no-man's-land of the vacations. Is it any wonder that, schooled in this way, we come in our maturity to accept ugly buildings, the closing of theatres, and the destruction of natural beauty in the countryside with little more than a murmur?

At least there are some modest signs of a gradual awakening to this responsibility for patronage. Music has come to be accepted in most British universities. Architecture and the fine Arts have established a firm footing here and there. Drama has made a start. Yet where writers are concerned, while every American university of any calibre can run a daily newspaper worth reading, we in Bristol have a struggle to publish two issues in a month. In America, of course, geographical isolation makes the need more urgent, or at least more keenly felt: but that does not excuse the lack of good writing here. It simply reveals that our students have nothing to say and that we have failed to stimulate them into finding anything.

It is my hope that the presence of a Fellow in Playwriting, and the existence of *New Theatre Magazine* within the Drama Department, will do something to redress the balance: but if we are to do our duty to drama as an art as well as to drama as a critical discipline, then we must do more than that. Here in Bristol I hope it will prove possible to strengthen our association with the Old Vic Company and School, and with the Little Theatre, and with the two broadcasting centres in the region. If medical students can be obliged to walk the wards of hospitals, or law students to sit in law courts and solicitors' chambers, I see no reason why students of drama should not occasionally be seen in theatres and in studios. And the same holds for staff. Better that both should occasionally be exposed to a little professional proficiency than cocooned perpetually in an esoteric atmosphere where amateur standards are transfigured into absolutes. If then we in Bristol do not exploit the remarkable facilities for co-operation with those many and varied interests in drama which exist in this city and with which history and luck have endowed us, we shall be judged by history as having thrown away an unique opportunity.

## VI

It is time now to draw together the several separate strands of my argument. I have looked at the twelve years of teaching experience which now lie behind us and have tried to single out from it what my colleagues and I have found to be the most worthwhile aspects of the subject. I then endeavoured to illustrate some of the ways in which the new subject could be used to advance the interests of both the individual student and the university. I stressed the power which the subject has to develop the personality of the student by balanced stimulation of intellect, enthusiasm, and creative capacity: and I dwelt upon the integrating qualities which the subject offers to a community where specialization has set up so many barriers and divisions between departments and faculties as to result in isolating one department and one faculty from another instead of binding them together as a co-ordinated whole. And lastly I have asked you to consider, within these terms of reference, the effects which the twin pressures of numerical expansion and the duty of patronage are likely to have upon any development of the subject in the years ahead. That said, it remains to state, as briefly as possible and in the broadest outline, the future I envisage for the subject.

I hope first that it will be possible to provide all students who read the subject with a swift canter through the entire range of drama as practised in the past, from the dance rituals of primitive peoples to the highly sophisticated and scientific media of presentation available today. After that to offer students at least three groups of special subjects in which they can develop their particular enthusiasms in a disciplined way. The first group would consist of the great dramatists and actors of the past—English and foreign, ancient and modern—from among whom they would select three or four to study and compare in detail. The second group would cover the quasi-scientific and archaeological aspects of the theatre—its buildings, perspective settings, principles of cinematography, and so on. The third group would cover the social aspects of the theatre—its economics, censorship, questions of status, and, above all, the critical opinion of society.

These options selected from within these three prescribed groups would be pursued consistently during the second and third years. Thus we could hope to offer students a discipline which extended their mental horizons during their first year in the department to the maximum extent, introducing them to Eastern as well as Western ways of thought and behaviour. That done, we could hope to offer them within this general framework a discipline in their second and third years which enabled them to penetrate selected aspects of the subject in depth as far as they were themselves capable of going. Throughout the whole three-year period we would require the student to engage in a limited amount of laboratory work of a strictly practical kind—again with a fairly wide range of choice. Central to the whole would be the obligatory critical study and constant debate of those moral values reflected in the varied dramatic history of different epochs and different peoples.

It will be seen that at post-graduate level this work can advance in two directions—the penetration in further depth of any academic subject matter, or the practical application of the lessons derived from it. I see no reason why there should not be room for both in the department, provided the two are not allowed to become confused with each other. I would not deny that a risk of confusion exists or that the price of such confusion is a decline in academic standards on the one hand and an esoteric professionalism on the other. This risk however is hardly more serious than that which others took in admitting this department into the university in the first place: and I cannot think that it would become me or my colleagues to forget the boldness of the example set us in the 1940's and flinch now when preparing to meet the needs of the 1960's.

I want therefore to see three types of post-graduate at work in the department. I want to welcome the M.A. or Ph.D. candidate who *knows* what he *wants* to study (as opposed to the kind who has to have a subject invented for him) and whose subject we can recommend to the Board of Faculty as one which will justify publication. In this context I am glad to be able to say that the department has been commissioned by a publisher to prepare in co-operation with other interested departments in this university *The Bristol History of European Drama* in some six volumes.

Alongside of higher degree candidates, I want to extend an equal welcome to post-graduates whose interest is avowedly vocational. Writers, producers, managers, critics, teachers—anyone who has proved himself or herself to be an able undergraduate here or elsewhere, and who knows what he wants to do with his life, will be welcome to join us for one year. The Certificate in Advanced Practical Studies, which I hope the university will agree to sanction in the near future, would be open to any graduates, whether in arts, science, or engineering subjects, who could convince us that their careers lay in the theatre, in films, television, or any other field where a humane approach allied to practical proficiency is at a premium. And in judging of this proficiency we would call upon the professional opinion available to us at the Old Vic, the Theatre School, and the B.B.C. In this way we could have confidence that the certificate was as acceptable a token of creative ability to professional practitioners as our higher degrees were guarantees of academic standing and capacity. And lastly I would hope to see the example of our earlier Rockefeller Lectures extended to enable selected artists of distinction to reside among us from time to time so that the discipline of experience may inform the discipline of study, and *vice-versa*. These, for me, are the proper paths for drama in a world shaped for us by science, and in which Man has come to regard himself as his own master.

If these paths are considered by you or by others to be no more than ideal dreams, well, let it be so. If these dreams fail to find fulfilment, then as Troilus put it:

'Hector is dead; there is no more to say.'

But should they be realized, then I think something will have been achieved for which not only the university but the city will be the richer. Adapting the title of the *Carmen Basiliense*, so splendidly set to music by Benjamin Britten as the *Cantata Academica*, and applying its ancient words to ourselves:

'Nos autem cuncti hoc festo die
Ex animi sententia
Optamus et precamur. . . .

We therefore together on this festive day
Wish to pray with all our heart
That a free academy may thrive
In a free community
For ever the ornament and treasure
Of illustrious Bristol.'

# IV

# *University Theatre*<sup>*</sup>

## I

THE small Italian town of Parma is noted among people interested in the theatre as being the place where the first proscenium-arched theatre was built in 1618—the *Teatro Farnese*, prototype of all theatre buildings in regular professional use until yesterday. When I visited this town last month, however, my purpose was not to see how the repairs to this war-damaged building were getting on, but to attend the IXth International Festival of University Theatre, organized by the University of Parma with full government and municipal support, moral and financial. Every night for a week a different play was presented in the splendid *Teatro Regio* by a different company. My own university of Bristol found itself sharing a playbill with the School of the Bolshoi Ballet Company, the Groupe Antique of the Sorbonne, Belgians, Italians, Jugoslavs.

Festivals of this sort have become almost a commonplace since the war. That at Parma is an annual event: so is the Festival of the European Students Union held at Erlangen, a German university town, between Nuremberg and Bayreuth. Another

* An Opening Address for the Annual Conference of the Society of Teachers of Speech and Drama, Nottingham University, April, 1961.

festival is organized biennially by the Delphic Institute of Mainz University. This was held in Bristol in 1959 and will be held at the University of Coimbra in Portugal this summer. Yet another festival, sponsored by the Turkish Government, is now held annually in Istanbul, usually in November.

The standard of performance as between one company and another and from one year to the next varies considerably: but this is probably of small importance compared to the general educational effects resulting from so much intermixing of European dramatic traditions. Not only do students see plays in performance which would otherwise remain textbook legends to them, but they see them performed by nationals versed in the national style appropriate to the dramatist's text: and, despite the barriers of language, post-mortem discussion can be informative as well as animated.

Another post-war development of equal interest, and for which the universities have supplied most of the initiative, is the formation of the International Federation of Societies for Theatre Research. Delegates from both sides of the Iron Curtain assemble annually in a city of their choice for a week's discussion of topics of mutual concern. London, Venice, Vienna, and Stockholm have all welcomed the conference, and this year it is to be held in Paris. It is usual to take a theme appropriate to the place of the conference—*Commedia del Arte* in Venice, *Court Theatres* in Stockholm—and for papers to be read by leading authorities on the subjects in question. A quarterly journal, published in French and English, keeps members in touch with one another through the rest of the year.

What strikes me as significant about this post-war activity is that means have suddenly come into existence for the scholar's interest in research and the practitioner's interest in performance to be pursued in an intelligent and co-ordinated international manner. And while the activities of the International Federation of Societies for Theatre Research are naturally of greater interest to dons than to students, students are not excluded: and similarly, while the Theatre Festivals are predominantly of concern to the student performers, members of staff are always made welcome and usually provide the most provocative contributions to the post-mortem discussions of the performances.

Scarcely less important for the future is the example provided by the growth of dramatic activity that has been going on in the U.S.A. Starting with the 'Workshop' established at Yale University by George Pierce Baker in 1919, the concept of drama as a lecture-room and examination subject has spread rapidly from coast to coast and from the Canadian border to the deepest South. In 1953 I visited a great many of the universities, large and small, in a whistle-stopping tour of the country. Last year I spent five months teaching in the Department of Speech and Dramatic Art in the State University of Iowa. Before heading west for Iowa I had time to pay a visit to Washington, D.C., in order to attend and to speak at the annual four-day convention of the American Educational Theatre Association with its membership of four thousand groups and individuals. This, too, runs its own quarterly journal.

As at the European festivals of which I was speaking, standards in American universities vary enormously between one department and another: and it does not by any means follow that the highest standards either of research or of performance are to be found in those departments which are most lavishly endowed and equipped. The money available in many of these institutions makes the English mind stagger. San Francisco State College has just been supplied with two theatres, workshops, and classrooms costing nearly two million dollars, and the University of California at Los Angeles is just starting to build plant estimated to cost sizably more than two million. It is true to say that every child in America with intelligence enough to find his way to high school or beyond who wants to learn something about drama and theatre has the opportunity to do so as an integral part of his studies.

It is a far cry indeed from conditions such as these to the situation in British universities and in the schools which feed the universities. Even so, the winds of change—of which we've heard so much recently in other contexts—have begun to blow a breath or two of novelty through the British scene as well. Bristol took the plunge with a Drama Department that awarded degrees in the Faculty of Arts in 1947; a Chair was established in 1960 and now Manchester has followed suit. Leeds, Nottingham, and Brighton are thinking of doing so, and rumour even attributes a similar intention to Cambridge. Southampton has commissioned Richard Southern to build them a theatre. Oxford has bought the Playhouse. The *Sunday Times* and the N.U.S. have joined hands to promote a competitive play festival each Christmas vacation, and the Royal Shakespeare Theatre has invited a number of university companies three summers running to disport themselves in Tudor and Stuart plays on the lawns of the theatre's gardens. Cambridge and Bristol collaborated (greatly helped by the Gulbenkian Foundations) to sponsor an international festival in England in 1959. So, whatever the attitude of academic authority may be to plays and players, there is no question but that student interest in the drama is more diverse and widespread than it has been since the days of the University Wits: and, more important, it enjoys proportionately greater power to influence, for good or bad, the development of the commercial theatre than it has ever done before.

## II

If most people are aware that many of the most publicized figures in the British theatre today are university graduates, few people, I venture to think, are aware how this has come about or have devoted much time to considering how this development is likely to affect the future of the theatre. In seeking to direct attention to this question now, I believe a better starting point is to be found in the wide, international context I have outlined than within the narrow limitations of a strictly national survey.

First of all, then, I think it must be admitted that the picture which I have endeavoured to present thus far displays a quite remarkable range of activity. Not so clear, perhaps, are the extremes of attitude within this range. The picture includes Russia and Germany, where even now amateur dramatics are regarded as incapable of possessing any merit which could recommend them to a paying public: but it also includes America and Commonwealth countries where, outside New York and respective capital cities, theatre (with rare exceptions) is amateur or does not exist. Between these extremes there are many compromises, several of them interesting in their own right. Take Turkey, for example. Here Western-style theatre is itself something of a novelty, and accordingly the framework of its organization is comparatively simple. The universities are the starting point, the seed-beds of talent. Talent manifested there is syphoned off and fed into what are called the Pocket Theatres: and it is from the State-assisted Pocket Theatres that the personnel of the fully subsidized State Theatres are recruited. Or take Italy. Most universities have an active dramatic society, but ninety-nine per cent of the membership have no professional pretensions whatsoever. Medicine, the law, teaching, and a variety of other vocations have already claimed them. Their dramatic activities are thus wholly recreational; and since there is no market outside university precincts for amateur dramatics of the kind which are so common all over Britain, the university societies tend to retain the loyalty and practical services of graduates, alumni, and junior members of staff. Artistic standards usually take second or third place in these circumstances to the perennial student pre-occupations of politics and wine, women and song: the university student seeking to make a theatrical career for himself will do so like his German-speaking neighbours as an assistant to a dramaturge. Only after years of watching the maestro has he any chance of working as a producer on his own account. In France two amateur dramatic societies, working within a very similar tradition, have acquired a national reputation (the *Groupe Antique* and the *Théophiliens* of the Sorbonne) as a result of confining their activities to highly specialized academic work performed in a highly professional manner.

In these circumstances it is scarcely surprising that the gap between what is understood by the words 'professional' and 'amateur' in respect of acting or any other theatre craft on the continent of Europe has a far sharper definition about it than is the case in this country or in America. In America it is often very hard to find any meaning in the use of either word. How can it be otherwise when Broadway actors who call themselves professionals are lucky to be in work for at most one-third of the year on average, while university students can be acting part after part through four years of undergraduate life and two or more years of graduate study besides being employed in every kind of technical capacity when not actually acting? Yet it is quite possible for this same student-actor to graduate with an M.A. in acting, having never had a voice lesson in his life nor considered it necessary to obtain control over his body for any purpose other than competing in athletic championships. Strangely, this is very far from true of American singers and dancers; nor is it too late to hope for reform where straight theatre is concerned.

The situation in this country differs in my experience from both that to the west of us in the States and that to the east of us on the continent. In the first place, unlike either the Americans or our neighbours on the continent, we cannot talk about 'the universities' as something uniform and consistent: we have to qualify the term 'university' with the epithets 'ancient' and 'modern'—that's if we're polite: there are other adjectives. Now whatever angry young Fabians care to say, drama at Oxbridge is one thing and drama at Redbrick quite another. The blunt truth is that for every six young men of outstanding histrionic talent at Oxbridge you are lucky if you find one in Redbrick. Where women are concerned this situation does not hold; but plays (especially the classics) tend to require more men than women for their performance. The difference is explicable partly as a matter of temperament, partly as a matter of background both at home and at school, partly as a matter of environment, and may be traced back to the Puritan Revolution of the seventeenth century: but it is also aggravated in the present by headmasters who proclaim the need for parity between the old and the newer universities but deny it by their actions. Headmasters and headmistresses compete with one another for prestige in their profession in terms of the number of scholarships they can secure at Oxbridge year by year. In this climate it is not surprising that Oxford and

73

Cambridge skim the cream and, in the process, take up the best histrionic talent. And who shall say that a boy is wrong to seek a place there? Or that his headmaster is misguided in pressing him to obtain it? Once the place has been won, the promising young actor quickly notices that the office of President of the O.U.D.S. or of the Marlowe Society is a matter for ambition if only because it appears to carry with it kudos comparable to that of winning a 'blue' or of office in the Union. No such honour attaches either in or outside Redbrick to the President of Dram. Soc. More than that, with its strong nonconformist and mercantilist traditions, Redbrick finds it hard to reward the flamboyance of the born actor's temperament with the tolerance accorded it at Oxbridge. Nor is there usually a personality of the Rylands-Coghill calibre around to protect and foster such unpopular fledglings. The aristocratic tyranny of Oxbridge patronage is the subject of much abuse today: but can any fair-minded person deny these patrons the credit for nurturing much of what our modern theatre is admired for both at home and overseas? Emlyn Williams, Michael Redgrave, Richard Burton, and Robert Hardy are among the actors of their school: Tyrone Guthrie, Norman Marshall, Peter Brook, Peter Hall, and Michael Benthal among the producers. If drama in British universities up to the present time has meant anything to the outsider, it has meant and still means the dramatic societies of these two universities, their patrons and their products.

You may say that the Coghill-Rylands tradition of drama in education is only an aspect of the much attacked 'establishment' and that the strings of former pupils who are now big names in radio, films, and television, as well as in the theatre, merely illustrate one strand of the old-boy network in action; that Stratford East is nowadays of more consequence than Stratford-on-Avon and the Royal Court more significant than the Old Vic, and you may well be right; but you must remember that George Devine, Tony Richardson, Lindsay Anderson, John Arden, and several others of note in those quarters, not to mention the founder of *Encore*, are all of the same school. And so, for better or worse, are the two professors of drama.

I am not disposed myself therefore to write off the Oxford and Cambridge tradition of according drama an extra-curricular status in a university as wholly erroneous or out of date: or, if I may phrase the matter another way, I am not prepared to argue that the American example of a fully fledged drama department is necessarily the right answer for every British university. Before I can admit that, I feel bound to ask the simple question, 'What does a drama department do for its students that they cannot do for themselves, granted facilities for the production of plays as an extra-curricular activity?' Part of the answer to that question is at once to hand in the inferior position which Redbrick dramatic activity has held up till now.

By virtue of historical circumstance Redbrick has developed in comparatively recent times out of colleges of commerce and technology, recruiting its students from sections of the population noted for their hostility or indifference towards the theatre. Dramatic activity, where it has flourished at all, was seldom undertaken before the war with any greater seriousness of purpose than house-party charades: and in those few instances when anything more worth while was attempted, the primitive nature of the production facilities successfully prevented reputations from growing beyond parish-pump dimensions. Only on the rarest occasions did notices of productions find their way into national newspapers. Changes in Redbrick recruiting since the war however, and in public attitudes to drama, have given the students of the modern universities their first opportunity to tackle plays in a manner which an objective outsider can take seriously. Anyone who has seen the work from Belfast, Birmingham, Leeds, London, or Durham that has appeared at any of the *Sunday Times*-N.U.S. festivals will admit that these universities possess some talent. It may not yet be talent of an outstanding order; and, numerically, it may still be in limited supply; but at least plays new and old that are intrinsically worth tackling are being regularly tackled, and there is evidence that the challenge implicit in such work has been found rewarding. Scrutiny of the past admits another ray of hope for the future, and of this I hesitate to say much since it concerns my own work at Bristol: but I think it only fair to my colleagues to state that with the establishment and growth of a drama department in that university both the range of theatrical activity and the standards of achievement have jumped spectacularly out of what I might describe as 'Third Division form' into Second Division if not yet into First Division class. Twelve to thirteen years is not a long time in the growth of a new institution, and as yet Bristol lacks anything that can be called a tradition: nor does it possess any prestige link-up with the professional theatre equivalent to the vigorous tendrils entwining Oxford with the London Vic or Cambridge with Stratford. That, however, may in itself be no bad thing, for we are now in the second half of the twentieth century and no longer in the first half: and it by no means follows that those patterns which were helpful to theatrical growth during the past sixty years are those which will automatically provide what is wanted during the next forty. Ever since *Look Back in Anger* received an almost unanimous verdict of disapproval from the press in 1956, only to grow into the most talked about theatrical event of the decade, there have been manifest signs of change in the theatre itself. And if the universities are to claim any further part in shaping the theatre of the future, may not they too have to reshape their attitudes and practices?

III

It is in considering the changes which are likely and desirable that I think we would be wise to take some notice of those continental and American patterns which differ from our own, and to which I have already called your attention: for the range of experience available to us from those quarters may as easily help us to recognize what we in this country should *not* do as provide ideas which we could copy with profit. The starting point, however, of any prognostication against the future, or of any planning, must surely be a serious consideration of both quality and purpose. Why should any dramatic activity be pursued in universities? Is the work being done at present as good as it could be? Is any of it positively harmful to the student or damaging to the theatre?

Judging from my own experience, the problem may be approached from three independent, if interrelated, standpoints: that of the professional careerist, that of the amateur enthusiast, and that of the academic historian. Paradoxical as it may seem, British universities have made fairly elaborate arrangements in the past to permit the performance of plays by students, but have refused to countenance any serious critical or historical appraisal of the theatre as a legitimate part of university studies. Most discussions of university drama have therefore been centred, willy-nilly, on the quality of performances—so and so's portrayal of *Coriolanus* or somebody else's production of *Electra* or *Les Mouches*. In this kind of discussion the edge of definition between amateur and professional acting quickly becomes blurred; and once that has happened the motives underlying all dramatic activity on an extra-curricular basis quickly become obscured by inflated personal opinion and proportionately exiguous attention to fact. Dons and students alike get into the habit of making direct comparisons between the version of a play presented by the student dramatic society and that given by a professional management. It is but a short step from here to making similarly direct comparisons between individual performances in specific roles. The danger latent in these comparisons is that of short-circuiting all questions of training and technique until it becomes possible to think of acting as something which anybody can do if so inclined. No musician would dream of playing an instrument in public without long hours of daily practice—scales, arpeggios, finger exercises, sessions with a metronome, and so on. Nor is this self-discipline simply a matter of attaining digital dexterity: rather is it a systematic training in how to develop the separate elements of melody, harmony, and counterpoint into a coherent ensemble fit to present to other people on a public occasion. Yet the student-actor has the effrontery to appear before public audiences with a voice and body over which he has little or no control and with virtually no training or experience behind him in working on a part. More often than not he will bring everything with which instinct has equipped him to the first reading of a play in order to create an impression among his fellow students.

77

Blind at the outset to the need to discover the elements of a character before attempting to realize them as an entity in terms of technique, he will remain blind throughout rehearsal or wake up to his deficiencies too late to remedy things. His performance can thus seldom amount to more than a two-dimensional penny-plain or twopence-coloured simplification of the character in question. Nevertheless he will have few qualms when it comes to charging the public for the right to see him act. Such impertinence (I'm sorry to use so strong a word, but the situation merits no less) is rivalled only by the student-producer who, without having learned how to act himself, sets himself up in the same relationship to actors as a conductor to musicians. Not knowing how to work on a part himself, he is incapable of teaching his tyro-actors how to do so. Instead, he subjects them to vague subjective waffle about 'the feeling of this scene', or takes refuge in equally subjective reflections about 'the author's intentions in these lines'. Thus, in a plethora of words, he confirms his actors in the ignorance of the amateur.

Students cannot be held wholly to blame for this state of affairs when they are clearly encouraged to progress in it by dons, friends, and relations and—where Oxford and Cambridge are concerned—by the mass attendance of national press critics: but much of the blame must nevertheless be squarely placed here for the debasement of the coinage of acting as an art in this country. When the universities mistake the amateur for the professional and encourage others to condone the mistake, no one should be surprised if the actor and his art are lightly regarded in municipal councils and government offices. It is all very well for the devotees of the theatre in this country to complain that we have no National Theatre, but it must be remembered that all those countries which do enjoy a State Theatre refuse to recognize amateur theatre as an activity warranting regular support at the box-office.

There is an important lesson here for Redbrick. Setting out, as so many of the newer universities are doing at the moment, on more adventurous and intelligent excursions into drama, are they to compete with Oxbridge for public recognition and press notices by the standards set in Oxbridge hitherto? Before this principle is allowed to develop as an axiom in default of any serious reappraisal of these standards, should we not pause to consider the advisability of encouraging yet more amateurs with graduate status to pose as professionals? Should university stage-triumphs continue to be regarded as qualifying students to act professionally or to direct other actors for financial reward?

## IV

It is always difficult to judge how much weight to attach to what professional actors have to say about producers and *vice-versa*. It is a fairly common experience to find actors refuting the credit given by press critics to the producer of a play and claiming that, but for their own exertions, the press and the public would have been confronted with an evening of unmitigated disaster. Indeed, when press critics have not attended any rehearsals it is very easy for them to place credit where none is due and *vice-versa*. Similarly, it is by no means unusual for producers to talk about what they have done or are going to do to a play in terms which suggest they have forgotten that it is the actors who will interpret between the play and the audience. It is, of course, part of the price that has to be paid for a free-enterprise, capitalist theatre, that all concerned in it professionally are placed under pressure to put press notices and other forms of personal publicity as first priorities; for they are all engaged in a fierce competition in which only the fittest today will be seen on that stage tomorrow. But even so it behoves us to enquire whether the success of so notably good a production as Stratford's *Titus Andronicus* is to be attributed to the producer's vision or to the actor's dominant role in it; or whether, when so notably bad a production as Stratford's *Othello*, starring Paul Robeson, is in dispute, the blame should be attributed to the actor or to the producer: for either way, good or bad, the actors in most instances are not university graduates and the producers are. Coupled with this is the growing suspicion— at least where Shakespeare productions are concerned—that some new 'gimmick' or other of presentation—Victorian dress,

Egyptian undress, exotic landscape, and so on—eclipses every-thing else in the minds of producers and the committees of management who appoint and employ them.

I do not myself object to gimmicks—without variety and change Shakespeare would quickly pall—but I do question the assumption that the gimmick is all, that it should take precedence over both the speaking of the text and the actor's contact with the audience: and I fear that where graduate producers are concerned, the gimmick often does take precedence for the simple reason that it can so conveniently conceal the producer's lack of know-ledge of actors and acting: in short, because he is an unskilled worker in the trade he is professing. It is as if a car manufacturer were putting a super-streamlined model into the Motor Show, oblivious of the fact that the mechanical parts inside the bonnet resembling an engine did not in fact work.

The dangers implicit in this situation have been mitigated in this country by the survival hitherto of a tradition of acting in-herited from a time when the actor was the master in his own house. Most of our leading actors and actresses have thus been equipped to hold their own and to retain the loyalty of the public: and on three occasions of note the ladies at least have exercised this power to force a show-down with the university wits. I have yet to hear of a man who is a match for Miss Littlewood; but she would not claim to be a university wit.

We are talking here, however, of a generation of actors and actresses—Richardson, Wolfit, Evans, and the like—whose active work in the theatre is nearing its close: and at the same time we are confronted with the rise of a new generation, whom Noel Coward cruelly nicknamed the 'scratch-and-mumble school' of acting, whose eyes seem to be more sharply focused on New York and Hollywood than on London or Stratford. And this, if my own experience of the American theatre is not misjudged, seems to me to be a profound mistake. For there, unquestionably, the actor has capitulated to the director (or, as we would call him, the producer). This would not be as serious as it is if the directors really knew something about acting: but with only the rarest of exceptions they do not. For the most part they are the products of university drama departments where, in everything other than strictly technical and mechanical skills, amateurs are training amateurs to train amateurs. All the basic professional craft of the actor has been forgotten, and there is no one around to repair the damage.

My point may be illustrated in the story of a young New York actor rehearsing in a Shakespeare play under an English actor-producer. Taken to task for massacring a line of verse he enquired in approved 'method' style where the character had come from and was stunned to receive the reply, 'Why, from off-stage, of course.'

I am not using this story to illustrate how a producer should treat actors, but simply to show what can happen when actors have forgotten what acting is. And if there is one thing that we in this country can do for the future of the English-speaking stage, it is to shout and shout and shout again that an actor is no actor until he knows how to command his own vocal instrument, how to comport himself on a stage, and how to command the attention of his audience. And if we can persuade actors who are actors in this sense to insist that producers are similarly trained, so much the better. If we fail, all the mumbo-jumbo of pseudo-science will drift like a fog into our theatres, blanketing the craft of acting in a tedious and unedifying spectacle of undisciplined behaviourism.

The same point may be illustrated from the other side of the fence. With my own university company in Parma last month I had a slight brush with the Russians. The Italian organizers of the festival in which we were participants had given the Russians a promise that they could have the stage every day of the week during the lunch-break. Unfortunately they had not told us of this promise. We were giving a 'first night' and had only one day in which to set up and deal with everything on the technical side from the lighting plot to dress rehearsal. In such circumstances there could be no lunch-break; and, in consequence, no stage for the Bolshoi Ballet School. I will not bore you with the miniature cold war of move and countermove which ensued. Suffice it to say that when the Russians realized that we would not risk the outcome of our first night by abandoning the stage to their routine exercises they agreed (with great charm) to a compromise which we had previously suggested but which they had declared to be unacceptable!

This little incident is trivial enough in itself: but the reason for its ever arising is not so trivial. These Russian students put in six hours of daily exercises even when theoretically 'on vacation' at a festival in the first city outside Russia which they had ever visited, and were not prepared in any circumstances to side-step this self-discipline even for one day. Their *strepitoso successo* with their audiences was thus not altogether fortuitous. In this country, dancers are normally subjected to the same rigorous discipline and so are opera singers. Is it possibly for this very reason that it is only at opera and ballet today that there lingers something of that former expansiveness of spirit implicit in the professional virtuosity of the performer, and the audience's readiness to accept the stylized conventions of presentation in which that virtuosity can sparkle? It is at least significant that metropolitan opera houses do not mount *Otello*, for example, unless a singer is available capable of sustaining the role, while no such scruples appear to trouble the managements of British theatres. Our theatre of stage-plays has become a dull, bourgeois affair, where even the Old Vic and Stratford smack more of Victorian pantomime than art, where great individual performances are now to be seen only on rare occasions spluttering erratically like a candle that is almost spent, and where a display of emotion in the auditorium is regarded as a form of impropriety if not of downright indecency.

As a theatre historian myself I cannot but be aware that the theatre of the past has been distinguished by three things—the sense of occasion surrounding performances, the esteem in which the public has held its favourite actors, and the quality of the plays written for them to perform and to grace these occasions. The producer or director is notably conspicuous by absence. It is inconceivable that a stage manager should not at all times have been an important person in dressing the stage for and with the actors. It is equally clear that with the tremendous advances made in the technical apparatus of modern theatres his role has become more important than it ever was in the past. It is this old-style stage-manager who has undergone a metamorphosis into the producer of modern times: at least this is the natural part of the change of state. A more artificial part of it is the change of social status that has accompanied it. And I cannot help feeling that the swelling tide of graduates who have found their way into the theatre in this capacity has played its part in creating this artificial and inverted relationship between the stage-manager and the actor which now characterizes the status of the producer: for the mere fact of being a graduate accorded to such producers a standing in a predominantly non-graduate profession which was based on social status rather than experience and merit. The rapid rise first of the cinema and then of television (where the director is necessarily in control) has served only to conceal the impropriety of this changed relationship, and to make what is essentially artificial appear natural. The growth of the amateur movement in this country has served to undermine the resistance that the professional actor might otherwise have offered.

As a person whose practical association with drama has been primarily that of a producer, I have had to search my conscience deeply before arriving at a conclusion so damaging to my own self-esteem; but I am now convinced that to assume, as many do, that universities should 'train' the producers of the future is very dangerous. For it can lead only to a gradual repetition in this country of the pattern which has so unfortunately become general in America. I say 'unfortunate' because the Americans have landed themselves in a position where it has become the job of the universities to train the actors as well as the producers: and this is a contradiction in terms. Universities cannot train actors. Acting, like singing and dancing, is an activity requiring constant exercise of voice and body, and an intimate knowledge of audience behaviour. This is a full-time occupation and one which must be tackled while body, voice, and mind have the flexibility of adolescence and before any of them have become damaged or set. Students enter university at eighteen, which is in general too late to begin, and are principally engaged while there in obtaining a degree based on critical study and written examinations—activities which eat up time in the preparation. Actors can of course survive a period of university life and pass on to a genuine theatrical apprenticeship in a theatre school or repertory theatre: Emlyn Williams, Miles Malleson, and Sir Michael Redgrave exist to prove the point, but for the majority who try to do so it will already be too late.

On the other hand, I think there is everything to be gained from exposing everyone who claims graduate status these days to some knowledge of those disciplines which underlie dramatic and theatrical art: for it is these graduates who are to become the patrons and the administrators of patronage of the future. In the most literal sense, the future of dramatic art in this country is in their hands. Is is thus of quite crucial importance that they should appreciate the need for it, the benefit to be derived from it—in other words, that they should be mentally equipped to fight for its preservation in a society where material self-interest is so rapidly eclipsing everything else.

It is within this context that I think the balance between Oxbridge and Redbrick in theatrical potential is beginning to shift in favour of Redbrick. The day of the extra-curricular dramatic society, of which the O.U.D.S. and Marlowe are our best examples, is not over: nor, I hope, will it ever be. For many medics, lawyers, engineers, and scientists, who are already committed to a career within their own subject, are thereby enabled as amateurs to enrich their social life and profit from a leisure recreation which is as interesting and informative as it is enjoyable. And who is to say that for many it does not have a therapeutic value as well! But the day has also arrived when the universities, having already usurped so large a measure of control in the professional theatre, can no longer be trusted to muddle along on an unthinking, unquestioning, ill-disciplined extra-curricular basis: for if they are allowed to do so I think they already have the power to destroy the theatre. A well-known actor recently said to me, 'Too many producers these days take an actor's performance from him'—in other words, they deprive him, by laboured explanation of a part, of the creative urge to act it. This actor's reaction is to hand the producer his wig. Once intellectual explanations come to be generally accepted as a substitute for technical proficiency, this attitude of a trained actor to an unskilled producer can very easily pass into becoming the attitude adopted by all first-rate actors to all their graduate patrons, managers, agents, and producers. And once the fatal words 'Do it yourself' have been shouted in an agony of despair and frustration from that quarter, then the rule of the amateur can begin, and dramatic art can disappear from our society as effectively as it did from that of the Roman Empire.

## V

This is the degree of danger, and this is where I think an officially recognized department of drama can serve as an effective breakwater against the sort of creeping paralysis that derives from both pretentious and well-meaning amateurism. A department, if properly organized, can establish the study of drama in such a way that an informed balance exists between instruction in historical fact, in critical theory, and in practical creativity. It can ensure that no instruction is given in practical theatre crafts (including acting and production) by anyone other than experienced professionals called in for that purpose. It can present students with a view of theatre as a civilizing influence in society, both in other centuries and among other peoples as well as in their own. It can equip teachers to communicate their own respect for dramatic art to children who may never go to a university, but upon whose support in their maturity the theatre must rely if it is to survive financially. And if it can provide industry with a regular supply of management trainees, it can also provide the theatre with the administrative brains that it so badly needs. Last but not least, by giving academic prestige to drama as a subject, a department can hope to raise general standards of printed and broadcast criticism substantially above the present level of gossip and personal opinion.

Radical change of this sort is something neither Oxford nor Cambridge can easily adjust themselves to constitutionally; and it is for this reason that I think that the great educational opportunity of the second half of the twentieth century, where drama is concerned, rests with the modern universities. For they have grown to maturity in a time when change is more normal than tradition, and they are acclimatized to adapting themselves to novelty. I do not myself advocate a fully fledged drama department under professorial control as necessarily the only answer for every university. In fact I would argue that no British university situated in a city or area of the country where a professional theatre of repute is lacking should establish such a department; for there the dangers of unbridled amateurism must always be too great to risk. In such places, however, the establishment of a readership or of a number of fellowships can serve just as well. For what the student dramatic society in the modern universities requires is continuity at staff level to offset the constant turnover of student personnel, and informed guidance in matters of dramatic art to offset the ineptitudes of the amateur theorists and enthusiasts. Those students of exceptional ability and enthusiasm can then go on after graduation to one of those universities where full-scale departments are established with facilities for post-graduate training in close collaboration with a professional theatre. Where these departments are concerned I am myself wholly opposed in principle to any policy which encourages members of staff who earn their appointments through academic attainment to suppose that they have any right *on that account* to be regarded as regular producers of student plays. This is plain feather-bedding. It creates an unhealthy situation in which the man who has chosen to teach because he has shirked taking all the risks implicit in a theatrical career, or has tried it and failed, can do untold damage to students who have no corresponding right to opt out. Where production is concerned, any measure of obligation that is imposed on students in a drama department to participate in practical work (as opposed to the voluntary participation normal to extra-curricular activity) is justifiable only if conducted by men and women whose qualifications pass muster with professionals. There is no intrinsic reason why the historian, critic, or theorist may not also earn recognition as a talented practising artist, and be appointed to the staff of a drama department on both counts: but the combination is rare. The most sensible solution to the problem is the one which accords most nearly with its facts: to accord full academic status to men and women with unexceptional academic qualifications in the subject, and part-time or 'special' status to those men and women without whose help the practical work obliged upon students would be open to exception. Granted conditions of this sort, the academic standing of university degrees can remain untarnished by spurious vocational and technological qualifications, while the professional actor can rest assured that the graduate entrant to the theatre is not a mere theorist hoping to rob the actor of his wig.

# V

# *L'Envoye*

AFTER those lectures when time allows for questions from the floor, I have found that no matter what my subject someone is likely to say, 'And what precisely *is* the relationship between the Drama Department of your university and the Old Vic Theatre and School in Bristol?' My answer runs: 'Officially, there is none. The Bristol Old Vic Theatre Company, the Bristol Old Vic Theatre School, and the Drama Department of the university are all autonomous, have separate premises, work under independent Heads, and are financially self-contained. Unofficially the connection is close.'

If the questioner wants further detail I take a deep breath and try to crowd some twenty years of history into three or four minutes.

The starting point is a building, the Theatre Royal in King Street: built in 1766, played by Sarah Siddons, Macready, Kean, and Irving, and now the oldest theatre in the country still in regular commercial use. Saved from threatened demolition and leased by the Arts Council to the Old Vic Trust, it has been the home of the Bristol Old Vic Company since 1943. Hugh Hunt, the first director of this company, founded a Theatre School to work in association with the company in 1945. Two years later the University of Bristol admitted drama as a degree subject within the Faculty of Arts.

88

To this extent, therefore, events have followed their own logic: the historic nature of the building suggested tenants appropriate to the building, the repertoire of the tenants allied to the comparatively small seating capacity of the building prompted the founding of the school; the existence of all three—building, company, and school—suggested that the University of Bristol was as good a place as any to pioneer the study of drama as a degree subject.

Once all three institutions were in existence each inevitably discovered that its own respective interests, however exclusive at first glance, overlapped at many points with those of its neighbours. Theatre history, for example, was the clear prerogative of the Drama Department. Yet, on closer examination, was this to mean that the school should have no truck with the theatre's historical past? Would this be proper for a school attached to a theatre and company so closely associated with the classical repertoire? Obviously not. Bodies. Who had first claim on the time of the students at the school? The theatre, for use as townsmen in *Romeo and Juliet*? Or the staff of the school for routine classes? Where should the theatre's archives be stored? On the spot, where no one had time or claimed to be qualified to look after them? Or in the University Library? Where should a promising young playwright be based, and who should finance him? At the Theatre Royal on an Arts Council Bursary, like Bernard Kops? Or in the Drama Department on a University Fellowship, like John Arden and Martin Shuttleworth? Who should give his play its try-out? University students? Acting students at the school? Or professional actors of the Old Vic Company? Costumes and scenery. Should such expensive equipment as this be bought and owned in triplicate? Or should it be pooled and shared?

Gradually, as the years have passed, these questions and many others like them have arisen in more or less acute form, have provoked some conflict of opinion, and have been answered in a way which has progressively diminished the clear-cut lines of demarcation defining the 'sovereignty' of the three institutions. Interdependence has come to replace independence. This has by now occurred on so many fronts that it is often difficult for the outsider to distinguish which institution is the prime contributor and the prime recipient in any particular enterprise.

This change has not come about without conflicts and crises. Theatre, school, and department have all been racked at one time or another (usually independently) by alarums and excursions of policy and personality: but somehow each has survived with all three somewhat clearer than they were before about one another's nature and capabilities. And classification has brought with it an additional measure of collaboration. One opportunity may have been lost. A building, instead of a mocking plaque, might well represent the National Theatre on the South Bank of the Thames by now if the Old Vic Trust had had sufficient faith in or understanding of its Bristol assets to foster their growth as organic parts of the parent company in London. Even the Moscow Arts and the Comédie Française could well envy a situation so organically well prepared to serve the needs and duties of a National Theatre as that which has existed in embryo within this English partnership: a school providing both a London and a provincial company with the majority of their hand-picked recruits, and a shuttle-service in the higher ranks of both companies to suit the requirements of their respective repertoires and the advancement of the actors, not to mention the expanding research and teacher-training until in the university concerned with the recruitment of the present and future audiences without which both Theatre Company and School are made redundant.

Perhaps it was asking too much of any company to expect the degree of imagination and determination required to seize this opportunity and to give it effective life, let alone to expect this of a company concerned with presenting a repertory of plays in London, New York, Moscow, and elsewhere. Certainly it is open to question whether any of the three Bristol units was sufficiently sure of its own individual function, or confident enough in the health and wealth of its partners, to have moved faster towards a coherent corporate relationship than has been achieved to date. If, however, an opportunity that has existed thoughout the past ten years or so has been lost, the particular compromise on the National Theatre issue adopted by the Government at least permits it to continue in existence: but there is a time limit, and that may be short. The Arts Council's lease of the Theatre Royal expires in 1963 and no one knows yet what will happen when this occurs: but it is greatly to be hoped that when this theatre celebrates its two-hundredth anniversary in 1966, Bristol will not have elected to disown its London cousins.

Some people may think that the future of the Theatre Royal is simply a question of preserving an historic monument and that it can be safely left to the Ministry of Works or the National Trust to deal with. Others may regard it as a matter of adjustment to the economics of the property market which must take its chance along with other buildings that are out of date in city centres. The more parochially minded may argue (if they are Londoners) that this theatre's future is merely one cultural item among many which is expendable because it is provincial; or (if they are Bristolians) that minimal subsidy from rates has already made it an issue for local party politics.

I would suggest, however, that what is really at stake is something much more far-reaching: the most promising answer offered thus far to all questions of theatrical training brought into existence by the breakdown of the actor-manager system some fifty years ago. The London academies and schools have attempted to provide a variety of answers: Oxford and Cambridge have made a substantial contribution through their respective dramatic societies: the theatre has itself supplied its own training schemes in provincial repertory, at the Old Vic and, more recently, at the Royal Court and the Theatre Royal, Stratford East. But time and experience have proved that all these answers have necessarily been partial, piecemeal, *ad hoc*, according to local and financial circumstance. What can now be offered by the theatrical interests that have developed in Bristol since the war, in partnership with the Arts Council and the Old Vic Trust, is a combination of everything that has proved to be profitable in what has been tried to date, coherently formulated within a neat, conveniently situated and flexible working relationship—repertory company, theatre school, university—all directly linked both to 'the best of the old and the best of the new' in buildings and repertoire, and to a notable London company. The location in Bristol of large radio and television studios (BBC and ITV) is another advantage of great contemporary significance.

My own belief is that dramatic art will continue to hold a place in a society shaped by science only if theatrical training, managerial and artistic, and the thinking behind that training, are adequate to the conditions of twentieth-century life. At the moment of writing the situation outlined above strikes me as in essence adequate to these conditions. If circumstances elsewhere are not so promising, that only means that the decisions which have to be taken in respect of the Theatre Royal, Bristol, within the next two years, may carry with them consequences out of all proportion to the size or value of the property concerned.

BRISTOL,
*October, 1961.*